presents

ASK THE PROS: SCREENWRITING

presents

Ask The Pros: Screenwriting

101 questions answered by industry professionals

Edited by Howard Meibach and Paul Duran

ASK THE PROS: SCREENWRITING
101 Questions Answered by Industry Professionals

LONE EAGLE PUBLISHING COMPANY
1024 N. Orange Dr.
Hollywood, CA 90038
Phone 323.308.3490 or 800.815.0503
A division of IFILM® Corporation, www.hcdonline.com

Printed in the United States of America
10 9 8 7 6 5 4 3 2 1

Cover design by Lindsay Albert
Book design by Carla Green

Library of Congress Cataloging-in-Publication Data

Ask the pros, screenwriting : 101 questions answered by industry professionals / edited by Paul Duran and Howard Meibach
        p.   cm.
    ISBN 1-58065-056-2
    1. Motion picture authorship. 2. Screenwriters—United States—Interviews. I. Duran, Paul. II. Meibach, Howard.

    PN1996.A78 2004
    808.2'3—dc22   2004046466

Select definitions taken from *The Filmmaker's Dictionary*, written by Ralph Singleton and James A. Conrad.

Books may be purchased in bulk at special discounts for promotional or educational purposes. Special editions can be created to specifications. Inquiries for sales and distribution, textbook adoption, foreign language translation, editorial, and rights and permissions inquiries should be addressed to: Jeff Black, Lone Eagle Publishing, 1024 N. Orange Drive, Hollywood, CA 90038 or send e-mail to info@loneeagle.com.

Distributed to the trade by National Book Network, 800-462-6420.

Final Draft® and Lone Eagle Publishing Company™ are registered trademarks.

ACKNOWLEDGEMENTS

This book wouldn't have happened without the support and encouragement from many people — especially my loving wife, Nancy, and my parents. They always believe in me no matter how silly I get. It's been a great ride. Every second of it. I knew that a book inspired by my Web site's "Ask A Hollywood Pro" forum would appeal to writers. Jeff Black at Lone Eagle Publishing agreed. He said, "Let's do it," before I even finished the pitch. If only it were that easy to get a movie deal. I have to thank Jeff and his wonderful partner-in-crime at Lone Eagle, Lauren Rossini, who put up with me and all my shenanigans.

Others for whom I am eternally grateful are: Tom McCurrie, my right hand man at Hollywoodlitsales.com, who has always been there when I need him; Paul Duran for his big contribution co-editing this book; the folks at Final Draft; Jesse Douma and Gabriele Meiringer at the Writers Store; Glynis Lynn at Phantom Four Films; Karin Cohen; Eva Peel, whose sage advice was so helpful; my wife Nancy, ace transcriptionist; and Chrissy Blumenthal at Escape Artists, who has been a friend of the Web site pretty much since its inception and who introduced me to many of the pros in this book.

Also, my hat is off to all the film industry professionals who took time out of their very busy lives to answer questions for this book. Each contributor pulled no punches in telling writers what they must hear.

—Howard Meibach
www.hollywoodlitsales.com

To the next generation of screenwriters — wherever they may come from, whatever age they may be. Keep your head down, your eyes and ears open, and your fingers moving.

And special thanks to those who have allowed me to do just that — Sara, Dexter, Ruby, and especially, my wife, Vera.

—Paul Duran

Lone Eagle Publishing would like to thank all of the people who so generously shared their time and expertise in answering questions for this book. In the process of "Asking the Pros," we learned a spectacular amount about the world of screenwriting. Of particular note are Gabriele and Jesse at The Writers Store, who contributed several excellent essays from their archives; Paul Duran, who came through for us all the way from Cuba; and our Lone Eagle authors: Linda Cowgill (*Writing Short Films, The Secrets of Screenplay Structure*), Peter Miller (*Get Published, Get Produced!*), Nancy Rainford (*How to Agent Your Agent*), and Linda Seger (*From Script to Screen, 2nd Edition*).

The Writers Store™, founded in 1982, is the world's foremost resource for software, books, continuing education and reference materials dedicated to writers and filmmakers. Specializing in story development, script processing, production and multimedia software as well as books and tapes, the West Los Angeles-based company has an award-winning Web site and free bi-weekly eZine, an international reputation for its user-friendly services and programs, and a long list of devoted clientele. www.WritersStore.com – 800.272.8927 or 310.441.5151

CONTENTS

INTRODUCTION

This book is the result of countless questions that Final Draft users have been asking us throughout the years, questions like "How do I get started in the business?", "What do I do when I finish my screenplay?", "Do I really need an agent and how do I get one?" We went straight to the Hollywood pros for answers to your many questions. Final Draft is more than just the industry-standard screenwriting software that Hollywood uses to write its film and television scripts. We have made it into a community, one that each and every Final Draft user is a part of. A unique community of highly imaginative writers, that everything and everyone in film and television needs as an integral part of The Big Picture. It all starts with the script. There are no studios without scripts. There are no power lunches or fancy suits without scripts. And without writers, there are no scripts. We at Final Draft remain dedicated to the writer. It has been my long-standing goal to right a wrong in Hollywood: the tradition that the writer is the bottom of the totem pole. Our aim in "Asking the Pros" was to show the writer, in an entertaining way, how to have a refreshing and invigorating swim in the shark-infested waters of Hollywood. Come on in, the water's fine.

Marc Madnick
Founder and President
Final Draft, Inc.

ASK THE PROS

PROFILES OF THE PROS

DINA APPLETON: Dina Appleton is Vice President of Business and Legal Affairs at Writers & Artists Group International, a talent and literary agency with offices in New York and Los Angeles. Dina is a member of both the Law Society of Upper Canada and the State Bar of California, and serves on the Beverly Hills Bar Association's Entertainment Law Executive Committee and the USC Entertainment Symposium's Planning Committee. She is the co-author of *Hollywood Dealmaking* with Daniel Yankelevits.

HAROLD BECKER: Harold Becker was a successful photographer in New York City before his directorial debut, *The Ragman's Daughter*, won the Giovanni Award at the Venice Film Festival. His next film, *The Onion Field,* established him as a master of the crime drama, and introduced James Woods, Franklyn Seales, and Ted Danson. He followed this up with *Taps*, a military drama that starred Sean Penn and Tom Cruise in memorable debuts. Other milestones in Harold Becker's career include *Sea of Love*, an erotic film noir thriller starring Al Pacino and Ellen Barkin; *Malice* a medical thriller with Alec Baldwin and Nicole Kidman; and *City Hall*, in which he teamed up again with Pacino. Other credits include *The Black Marble*, *Vision Quest*, *Mercury Rising*, *The Boost*, and *Domestic Disturbance* with John Travolta and Vince Vaughn.

CHRISSY BLUMENTHAL: Producer Chrissy Blumenthal began her career as a story editor at Mandalay Entertainment. In 1999 she joined Todd Black and Jason Blumenthal's Black and Blu Entertainment as Vice President of Development, overseeing the production of such films as *A Knight's Tale* and *Antwone Fisher*. In 2001 Black and Blu merged with the Steve Tisch Company to form Escape Artists, which is currently in pre-production on *Weather Man*, directed by Gore Verbinski and starring Nicholas Cage; as well as *Need*, directed by Marcus Nispel and starring Diane Lane. As Senior Vice President of Escape Artists, she is personally overseeing the development of Thompson Evan's romantic-comedy, *Wedlocked*, starring Meg Ryan; and an adaptation of Karyn Bosnak's novel, *Save Karyn*.

MARTI BLUMENTHAL: Marti Blumenthal has been a literary agent in the motion picture and television industry for over fifteen years. She currently is a partner and oversees the literary department at Writers and Artists Group International, which encompasses both motion pictures and television. Some of her personal projects include raising the financing for *Igby Goes Down* and negotiating the sale of film rights to many of John Grisham's best-selling novels. She is co-founder of Showbiz Seminars, a company established to educate the next generation of screenwriters and filmmakers about the industry. She is also a member of the Academy of Motion Picture Arts and Science.

MARTY BOWEN: Marty Bowen is partner and agent at the United Talent Agency.

LARRY BRODY: A television writing legend, Larry Brody has written and/or produced and created thousands of hours of network television programming, including such animated series as *Spawn, The Silver Surfer,* and *Spider-Man Unlimited*; as well as primetime series such as *Mike Hammer, Baretta, Medical Story, The Fall Guy, The Streets of San Francisco,* and *Police Story.* Brody has won or been nominated for every major television award and both *Spawn* and *Police Story* have won Emmys for Best Series. Brody is also the Founder and Creative Director of Cloud Creek Institute for the Arts, a non-profit corporation dedicated to advancing the arts by helping new artists get a foot in the door. Brody has used his award-winning Web site, tvwriter.com, to help launch the careers of many new writers, and his book, *Television Writing from the Inside Out: Your Channel to Success*, is a top seller.

STANLEY M. BROOKS: Veteran TV Producer Stanley Brooks started his career as Vice President of Development for Centerpoint Productions, where he developed *Oceanquest*, an NBC documentary miniseries that garnered five Emmy nominations. Brooks left Centerpoint to become President of Guber-Peters Television, which afforded him an opportunity to help some of the more prominent writers and producers in television to move into features, the foremost example being Barry Morrow with *Rain Man*, which went on to win Best Picture in 1988. After Brooks left Guber-Peters, he started Once Upon A Time Films, and embarked on a series of TV firsts: producing MTV's first movie, *Jailbait!*; TNT's first MOW, *Finish Line*; and Arnold Schwarzenegger's directorial debut *Christmas in Connecticut*. Last year, his company produced the first telefilm to ever air on ESPN: *A Season on the Brink*, starring Brian Dennehy as former Indiana head basketball coach Bobby Knight. This year Once Upon A Time Films has already produced three TV films including *Beautiful Girl* for Disney; *On Thin Ice* with Diane Keaton for Lifetime; and *The Legend of Butch & Sundance* for NBC.

LINDA COWGILL: Linda Cowgill is a screen and television writer who has taught at the AFI, the Kennedy Center, the Boston Film Institute, Loyola Marymount University, and the LA Film School. As a student at UCLA, she won a Jim Morrison Award for best short film, and in 1986, her feature film, *Opposing Force*, was released by Orion Pictures (under a pseudonym). She has written for such television shows as *Quincy*, *The Young Riders*, and *Life Goes On,* for which she won a Genesis Award. Ms. Cowgill teaches a seminar called *The Art of Plotting*, and is also the author of *Writing Short Films* and *Secrets of Screenplay Structure.* Her Web site can be found at www.plotinc.com.

LISA CRON: Lisa Cron spent a decade in publishing as an editor and publicist before turning to writing. On the strength of her spec script, *Overnight Sensation,* she was hired by producers Brett and Bill Hudson (Kate's dad) to write the pilot and bible for a one-hour family drama they were developing. She spent the next seven years commuting between New York and Los Angeles, where she served as a writer and producer on several projects with Hudson. In New York she was a story analyst, first for Warner Bros., then for the William Morris Agency, concentrating on books to film. She has read for such companies as Miramax, Icon Productions, Village Roadshow, and the Don Buchwald Agency. As a natural off-shoot of her work, about ten years ago she also began working one-on-one with writers, as a literary coach.

MARK DEMPSEY: Mark Dempsey is currently a freelance story analyst. Prior to that, Mark was a development executive at Echo Lake Productions for seven years, where he was Vice President and Director of Development. During his tenure at Echo Lake, Mark evaluated submissions, advised the company on the acquisition of new projects, and assisted in the development of many of Echo Lake's current slate of projects. Mark is a graduate of Southern Methodist University and received his MFA in Screenwriting from Loyola Marymount University.

DIANE DRAKE: Diane Drake's credits include the Paramount romantic comedy *What Women Want* starring Mel Gibson and Helen Hunt; and *Only You*, directed by Norman Jewison, and starring Robert Downey, Jr. and Marisa Tomei. Before turning to screenwriting full time, Drake was Vice President of Creative Affairs for Director-Producer Sydney Pollack's Mirage Productions. She is a native of Los Angeles, and earned a Bachelor of Arts degree from the University of California at San Diego.

DAVID ENGEL: David Engel is a partner at the West Coast office of the management/production company, Circle of Confusion. Circle has a first-look production deal with Columbia Pictures. Additionally, the outfit manages such film, television, and comic book clients as The Wachowski Brothers (*The Matrix* trilogy), Simon Kinberg (*XXX2*), Chabot & Peterka (*Reign of Fire*), Kiran (*Kid Bang*), Brian Michael Bendis (*Spider-Man, Powers, Jinx*), Michael Avon Oeming (*Hammer of the Gods, Bastard Samurai*), Dan Brereton (*The Psycho, The Nocturnals*), and James Hudnall (*The Psycho, Harsh Realm*). Formerly, Engel was Director of Development for Mace Neufeld Productions, where he discovered *Powers*, the graphic novel now set up at Sony, and previously found the comic book *Harsh Realm,* which aired on Fox TV.

4

JOHN FASANO: Moving to Los Angeles in 1990 John Fasano sold his first script, *Tailgunner,* to Morgan Creek for $1.5 million. Other feature films followed in quick sucession: *Another 48 Hours* (Paramount), *Judge Dredd* (Cinergi), *Universal Soldier: The Return* (Columbia), and 2003's *Darkness Falls* (Columbia). Additonal screenplay sales include *Shaolin* for Disney, and *Werewolf By Night* for Marvel Comics/Dimension Films. Fasano also had a role in producing the motion pictures *Darkness Falls* and *Tombstone* (Hollywood Pictures), as well as creating several television pilots and telefilms including *FX: The Series* for Rysher, *Mean Streak* for Showtime; the miniseries *The Forever War* for the Sci-Fi Channel; *The Hunley* and WGA-nominated teleplay *The Hunchback,* both for TNT; *Christine Refuelled, Saving Jessica Lynch,* and *The Legend of Butch and Sundance* for NBC. John is represented by ICM and Baumgarten Management and Production.

ROBBIE FOX: Robbie Fox studied theater and film at Northwestern and New York Universities. His short film *The Great O'Grady* won several comedy awards on the festival circuit and played for several years on Showtime. He wrote the original feature film comedies *So I Married an Axe Murderer* with Mike Myers, and *Shooting Elizabeth* with Jeff Goldblum, as well as the story for *In the Army Now* with Pauly Shore. He's done punch ups on various TV shows and movies including the Disney short *Runaway Brain,* and *My Girl* with Dan Aykroyd and Macaulay Culkin. For the theater, he wrote *The Gift,* a musical starring Alicia Witt that played in Los Angeles during the summer of 2000. Two years before that he did the New York workshop of that musical under Herbert Ross' direction, then called *Complications.* He currently has a number of original scripts in development with Disney, Fox, and Universal. His next two films are romantic comedies: *Once in Love with Jamie,* which is currently casting to be produced in 2004 by One Roof Entertainment, and *So I Met This Girl,* which will be directed by Joel Zwick.

DAVID T. FRIENDLY: David T. Friendly has been a producer and executive in the film business for over thirteen years. Friendly began his career as a journalist at *Newsweek* and later at the *Los Angeles Times*, where he was approached by Imagine Entertainment co-founders Brian Grazer and Ron Howard to join their company. During seven years at Imagine, he rose to President of Production and was integral to many of the company's hits, including *Backdraft, Kindergarten Cop, The Dream Team,* and *The Burbs,* and served as Executive Producer on *My Girl, Greedy,* and *The Chamber.* In 1994, Friendly joined Davis Entertainment as President, where he oversaw all aspects of development and production. In 2000, Friendly teamed with Marc Turtletaub to form Deep River Productions. Bankrolled at upwards of $25 million, this new production entity will finance its own development and overhead, while partnering with various studios. He is currently finishing *Laws of Attraction,* starring Pierce Brosnan and Julianne Moore. His other credits include *Big Momma's House, Here on Earth, Dr. Doolittle,* and *Courage under Fire.*

D.B. GILLES: D.B. Gilles is the author of the popular screenwriting book, *The Screenwriter Within,* published by Random House. He teaches Screenwriting and Comedy Writing in the Film Department at New York University. He also teaches in the Graduate Film Department at Columbia University. He writes a weekly column on screenwriting for Hollywoodlitsales.com and also writes for writerstore.com. Mr. Gilles is a script consultant who can be reached directly at dbgilles47@aol.com.

BARRY GOLD: Barry Gold is a TV writer who has written for *Arliss, Major Dad,* and *Family Matters,* as well as several other sitcoms.

KIRA GOLDBERG: Kira Goldberg is the Head of Development at Lynda Obst Productions.

DAVID GOYER: Writer-Director-Producer David S. Goyer began his writing career soon after graduation from film school at USC, with the Jean-Claude Van Damme starrer *Death Warrant,* followed by three more produced features and the NBC series, *Sleepwalkers.* After writing New Line's comic book-to-film hit *Blade,* and the haunting, noirish *Dark City,* David co-produced Disney's *Mission to Mars* while creating and writing the Fox series, *Freakylinks.* He also wrote and executive produced *Blade II* and adapted *Murder Mysteries,* a supernatural thriller based on a short story by Goth comic book guru Neil Gaiman. Recently David wrote the comic book *JSA* for DC comics, adapted Jeff Long's novel *The Descent* for DreamWorks, and wrote the intensely anticipated *Batman* for director Christopher Nolan. *ZigZag,* David's directorial debut, allowed him to launch his own production company, Phantom Four Films, through which he will produce the ghost story *Alone* for New Line Cinema, the futuristic comic *Y: The Last Man* for New Line, and the science-fiction-themed comic *Unique* for Touchstone. Currently, David is directing his second feature, *Blade III*, on which he also serves as producer and writer.

GRADY HALL: Writer-Director Grady Hall's industry experience ranges from the mailroom to the director's chair. He started his career at Warner Bros., and read thousands of scripts on the way to becoming, at age twenty-five, the head of development for a prolific television producer. Grady worked on his own movies and series projects, eventually staffing *The Outer Limits* for Showtime. More recently, he has written and directed music videos for bands such as R.E.M. and Less Than Jake, and directed commercials for Nike, DIRECTV, McDonalds, ESPN, and others.

JONATHAN HANDEL: Jonathan Handel is Of Counsel at the Troy & Gould law firm in Century City, where he practices entertainment and digital media law. He was previously Associate Counsel of the Writers Guild of America. Mr. Handel serves on the Business and Management Advisory Board of UCLA Extension's Entertainment Department, and has taught film appreciation classes and seminars on entertainment law, business, and technology. The material presented here is for general information only. It is not legal advice, and may not represent the views of the organizations listed. His Web site is www.jhandel.com.

RIO HERNANDEZ: Rio Dylan Hernandez is a recent graduate of USC's Master of Professional Writing Program. She has worked both in film production and development, and been a script analyst for such companies as DreamWorks SKG, New Line, Tri-Star TV, and the William Morris Agency.

JON HUDDLE: Jon Huddle is a motion picture literary agent at ICM.

CLAUDIA JOHNSON: Claudia Johnson and Matt Stevens are the co-authors of *Script Partners: What Makes Film and TV Writing Teams Work*, the first book on the subject of collaborative scriptwriting. Claudia is also the author of the popular film school text *Crafting Short Screenplays That*

Connect, and *Stifled Laughter*, which was nominated for the Pulitzer Prize. Their Web site can be found at www.scriptpartners.com.

LARRY KARASZEWSKI: Larry Karaszewski is the writing partner of Scott Alexander. Together, they wrote *Ed Wood*, for which they were nominated for Best Screenplay by the Writers Guild of America. They followed this with *The People vs. Larry Flynt*, for which they won the Golden Globe for Best Screenplay, as well as a special Writers Guild Award given in recognition of work done for civil rights and liberties. They re-teamed again with director Milos Forman on *Man on the Moon*, a biopic about the legendary comic genius Andy Kaufman. They currently are writing and directing a biopic on the Marx brothers. Collaborators since their senior year at USC's School of Cinema, they began their careers with the box office hit *Problem Child* and its sequel.

KEN KOKIN: Ken Kokin is a producer whose credits include *The Way of the Gun*, *The Usual Suspects*, and *Public Access*. He is a graduate of the USC School of Cinema-Television.

ADAM KOLBRENNER: Adam Kolbrenner began his career in the mailroom at the William Morris Agency in New York, and ended up working for legendary music agent, Jon Podell, and such clients as The Eagles, Peter Gabriel, The Allman Brothers, and dozens of hip hop artists. He was also responsible for client bookings of summer tours and festivals including Woodstock '94, Lollapollooza, and the Horde Festival. Later he moved to William Morris' offices in Los Angeles where he worked in both motion picture and television packaging with such high profile clients as John Travolta, Candice Bergen, Elaine May, Dustin Hoffman, and Arnold Schwarzenegger. At the age of twenty-four, Adam became the co-founder of Foundation Management, and is currently head of literary management and co-head of productions. Under the FLM banner, Adam represents over thirty working writers and directors for film and television.

GREGG MCBRIDE: Gregg McBride is a screenwriter and TV writer whose credits include *Have a Nice Life* for MTV Films and *Happily Never After* for Disney. He was also a staff writer on MTV's hip, sexy series *Undressed*.

PETER MILLER: Peter Miller has been a literary and film manager for over thirty years. He has represented over 900 books and has had eleven New York Times bestsellers, and eleven movies produced that he either managed, developed, or executive produced. As a producer, he has been nominated for two Emmy Awards. His company, PMA, is based in New York, but he stays in close contact with Los Angeles-based studio, network, cable, and film company executives as well as with West Coast-based agents, managers, screenwriters, and directors. PMA also employs foreign representatives throughout the world since many of their clients have been global bestsellers. PMA's sister corporation, Millennium Lion, Inc., is a production entity that coordinates the submission of all potential film properties to television networks, studios, and production companies. You can contact Peter Miller through his company's Web site at www.pmalitfilm.com.

CRAIG MOSS: Craig Moss is part of a screenwriting duo that includes Steve Schoenburg. Together they have written *Night Girls* for New Regency, *National Lampoon's Back to College*, and *Sissymarys* for Universal. Their TV work includes *Crank It Up* for Fox, and *Feltlyn* for Fox and the WB.

WENDI NIAD: Former literary agent Wendi Niad opened Niad Management in 1997 with the goal of providing close personal advice and counsel for her carefully chosen stable of writers and directors. She began her career at ICM working with heavy hitting clients and companies such as Roland Joffe, Randall Wallace, 40 Acres and a Mule, and Stephen J. Cannell Productions.

STEPHANIE PALMER: Stephanie Palmer is currently the Director of Creative Affairs at MGM Pictures. Originally from Alexandria, Virginia, Stephanie received a B.F.A. in theater directing from Carnegie Mellon University. Her first job in the business was as an assistant at Jerry Bruckheimer Films on *Armageddon* and *Enemy of the State*. She has worked at MGM since 1999 where she started as an assistant and has been promoted three times to her current position as a development and production executive. In 2003, she was named one of the "Top 35 Under 35 Entertainment Executives" by *The Hollywood Reporter*.

DENNIS PALUMBO: Formerly a Hollywood screenwriter (*My Favorite Year; Welcome Back, Kotter*), Dennis Palumbo, M.A., MFT, is a licensed psychotherapist in private practice, specializing in creative issues. He's the author of a novel (*City Wars*), as well as numerous articles and reviews. His most recent book is *Writing From the Inside Out: Transforming Your Psychological Blocks to Release the Writer Within*. Dennis' work helping writers has been profiled in *Premiere, GQ,* and the *Los Angeles Times,* as well as on CNN. His Web site can be found at www.dennispalumbo.com.

PARIS QUALLES: Known primarily for his work as an episodic and long form television writer-producer, Paris Qualles spent more than fifteen years in the theater as an actor and director before turning to film and television writing. His episodic television credits include *China Beach, Equal Justice; Lois & Clark, The New Adventures of Superman; Quantum Leap, Law & Order, Amen,* and *The Heights.* Television movies include the Emmy-winning *The Cape*; the Emmy, Cable-ACE, Image, and Peabody award-winning *The Tuskegee Airmen*; the Cable-ACE winning *The Ditchdigger's Daughters*; and the Emmy, Writers Guild, Humanitas, and Image award-winning *The Color of Friendship*. Other TV movies include *The Rosa Parks Story*, *Profoundly Normal*, and *Standing at the Scratch Line*. Feature films include *The Inkwell, Brothers, Hannibal,* and *Sadgwar*. Paris has received a Humanitas Award, Writers Guild Award, Image Award, and Christopher Award.

PAT QUINN: Pat Quinn is a literary and packaging agent at Innovative Artists. She is one of the top packagers in the entertainment industry with a background in television production, feature films, and theater. Her client list includes award-winning screenwriters, primetime comedy and drama series show runners, and production companies. She is also an instructor at UCLA Extension, creating the courses "Pitch Like the Pros: Insider Tips for Selling Your TV Show"; "Agent Representation for Film and Television Artists"; "Pilot Season: Packaging, Pressure, and Perseverance"; and "Who Wants to Be a Millionaire? A Guide to Developing, Selling, and Producing Reality/Alternative TV Programming."

NANCY RAINFORD: After graduating from SUNY, Purchase, Nancy Rainford began her career in New York reading scripts for a Broadway producer. In search of warmer climates, she moved to Los Angeles and spent nine years as a talent agent, representing actors, writers, and soon-to-be directors. She then switched hats from seller to buyer and began four years of television and feature film casting, including over twenty television series and pilots for ABC, NBC, CBS, Fox, and HBO. Today, as a manager and producer, she handles writers, actors, and directors, and is currently developing projects for theater, television, and film, including Tim Ryan's critically acclaimed one-man show *All the Help You Need*.... Together with client Hopwood DePree, she co-created and executive produced *Dear Doughboy,* a half-hour comedy pilot originally shot for the WB network and Brillstein-Grey Productions. Rainford's book, titled *How to Agent Your Agent*, was written for actors, writers and anyone who finds themselves in need of representation.

DYANN S. RIVKIN: Dyann S. Rivkin is an award-winning writer-producer of broadcast network, nationally syndicated, and cable television programs; entertainment, educational, and promotional videos; and films. Her background includes ten years of Los Angeles production and scriptwriting experience as well as filming on location across America, and in Canada and Ireland. She has taught video production at Vanderbilt University and has taught screenwriting at Belmont University in Nashville, where she also teaches private courses in the art and craft of screenwriting.

MYRL A. SCHREIBMAN: Myrl A., Schreibman, author of *The Indie Producers Handbook: Creative Producing From A-Z*, has been a producer for over three decades and a faculty member of the UCLA Film School. He has produced and/or directed award winning projects for theater, film, and television, both on the studio level and the independent level. One of the leading authorities in the field, his lectures on producing and directing have inspired the likes of Producer Dan Angel (*Door to Door*), and Director Justin Linn (*Better Luck Tomorrow*). His theories on producing are now studied at all the major film schools in the United States. His Web site, www.indieproducing.com, is one of the most visited sites of its type on the Internet.

ARNOLD SCHULMAN: Arnold Schulman sold his first story at age ten and ever since has thought of doing nothing else but writing. He started out as an aspiring playwright, studying form and structure with Clifford Odets and others. He received on-the-job training in New York as a writer for live television and worked on nearly seventy teleplays. Eventually, Schulman was beckoned to Hollywood by Director George Cukor and Producer Hal Wallis to write *Wild is the Wind*. Some of his other screenplay credits include *Funny Lady, A Chorus Line* and *Tucker: A Man and His Dream*. In addition, he has two Oscar nominations, one for Best Original Story and Screenplay (*Love with the Proper Stranger*), and one for Screenplay Adaptation (*Goodbye, Columbus*). He also has three Writers Guild nominations for Best Screenplay (*Wild is the Wind, A Hole in the Head,* and *Love with the Proper Stranger),* and a Writers Guild Award for *Goodbye, Columbus.*

SETH SCHUR: Seth Schur is Director of Development for Saturn Films, where he heads up development for the company's project slate, including coverage and story notes, and is responsible for all new material. Seth started out as an administrative assistant at Stone Meyer & Genow, LLP, working with the company's entertainment attorneys on contracts for talent and literary clients. In 2000 he moved over to Saturn, where he oversaw production on *The Life of David Gale* and *Sonny*. Seth was also a juror at the Los Angeles International Short Film Festival in 2002.

LINDA SEGER: Dr. Linda Seger defined the job of script consultant in 1981, when she began her script consulting business based on a system for analyzing screenplays that she developed as part of her doctoral dissertation. She has consulted on over 2000 projects, including over thirty produced TV projects, and over fifty produced feature films. Her clients have included TriStar Pictures, MGM/UA, Guber-Peters Entertainment, and Charles Fries Entertainment, as well as Ray Bradbury, William Kelley, Tony Bill, Dave Bell, Linda Lavin, and Suzanne De Passe. She is the author of seven books on screenwriting and filmmaking: *Making a Good Script Great; Creating Unforgettable Characters; The Art of Adaptation: Turning Fact and Fiction into Film; From Script to Screen: The Collaborative Art of Filmmaking* (with co-author Edward Jay Whetmore); *When Women Call the Shots: The Developing Power and Influence of Women in Television and Film;* and *Making a Good Writer Great, Advanced Screenwriting: Raising your Writing to the Academy Award Level;* and her latest release, *From Script to Screen: The Collaborative Art of Filmmaking, 2nd Edition,* also written with Edward Jay Whetmore.

PROFILES OF THE PROS

CHARLES SHYER: In 1979 Charles Shyer and Nancy Myers teamed up to write *Private Benjamin*, which they also produced. The screenplay won Meyers and Shyer a Writers Guild of America Award for Best Original Screenplay and was nominated for an Academy Award in that same category. The film was also nominated for multiple Golden Globe Awards, including Best Picture and Best Actress. Shyer's next project, *Irreconcilable Differences*, marked his directorial debut. In 1991, Meyers and Shyer remade the 1950 Vincente Minnelli classic, *Father of the Bride* (with Shyer directing) and later its sequel, *Father of the Bride, Part II*. Shyer is currently in post-production on a film based on the 1960s classic, *Alfie*. The new version stars Jude Law and is scheduled for a fall/holiday 2004 release.

MATT STEVENS: Matt Stevens and Claudia Johnson are the co-authors of *Script Partners: What Makes Film and TV Writing Teams Work*, the first book on the subject of collaborative scriptwriting. Matt is a writer-director-producer who has sold both fiction and documentary projects and is a contributing writer for E! Online and numerous new-media outlets. Their Web site can be found at www.scriptpartners.com.

DAN STRONCAK: Dan Stroncak has spent a decade working in the entertainment industry. After graduating from the UCLA Professional Screenwriting Program he worked as a development assistant for 20th Century Fox, then as a casting associate for Valerie McCaffrey. He learned feature film finance as a foreign distribution consultant for Morgan Creek Productions, then returned to development as a story analyst for Intermedia Films and Shady Acres Entertainment. He was also a creative executive for Director Steve Anderson, a VP of Development for Blue Raven Films, and an associate producer with Bogorad/Wyler Productions, before establishing Exemplar Entertainment, a literary management and independent production company. Currently Dan is working as a creative executive for producer Christine Peters (*How To Lose A Guy In 10 Days*) at Paramount Pictures.

STEPHEN SUSCO: Stephen Susco has been a screenwriter since 1996. He has written scripts for New Line, Universal, Dimension, Sony, Miramax and Paramount Studios, and for directors and producers such as Mike Nichols, Quentin Tarantino, Ted Demme, Gale Anne Hurd, Philip Noyce,

Taylor Hackford, Sam Raimi, and John Leguizamo. His first produced film, *The Grudge*, will be completed this year.

DAVID TROTTIER: David Trottier is the author of *The Screenwriter's Bible* — now in its third edition — which contains the latest on formatting, spec style, script marketing, writing guidelines, and more. In his capacity as screenwriter and script consultant, he has developed projects for, among others, the Walt Disney Company, Jim Henson Pictures, New Century, and York Entertainment. More information on Trottier can be found on his Web site at www.keepwriting.com.

JOHN TRUBY: John Truby has taught his *Great Screenwriting* and *Genre* classes to over 20,000 students worldwide. He has been a story consultant and script doctor for Disney Studios, Sony Pictures, FOX, HBO, Alliance Atlantis, Cannell Studios, BBC, and others. His *Blockbuster* software takes students through the entire writing process using his award-winning "22 steps of every great story." You can visit his Web site at www.Truby.com.

CHRISTINE VALADA: Christine Valada, Esq. is a copyright and entertainment lawyer practicing in Los Angeles County, California. She represents individual writers, visual and performing artists, and is California Legislative Counsel for the American Society of Media Photographers. From 1996-2002 she served as outside general counsel for the Science Fiction and Fantasy Writers of America. She graduated from Case Western Reserve University School of Law and clerked for both the Writers Guild of America, west, Inc. and the Directors Guild of America, Inc. during two successive summers. She has a special interest in creators' rights and her article "Truth, Justice, and the American Way" about comic book properties and the law was the cover story for a past entertainment law issue of *Los Angeles Lawyer* magazine.

DOUG WALLACE: Doug Wallace is a screenwriter who has written and developed projects for Gail Anne Hurd, Phillip Noyce, Arnold Kopelson, Jon Peters, Michael Phillips, Alan Riche, Tony Ludwig, Doug Wick, CZ Wick, Neil Moritz, Brad Luff, Ricardo Mestres, and Channing Dungee, among others. He has also written for the TV series *Monsters* and *Tales From the Dark Side*, and he wrote the feature film *Sensations*, which premiered on HBO in 1995.

DANIEL YANKELEVITS: Daniel Yankelevits is an executive in the Business and Legal Affairs Group at DreamWorks SKG, and teaches an annual entertainment law seminar at UCLA. He previously served as Director of Business Affairs at HBO and at New Line Cinema, and was co-chair of the Beverly Hills Bar Association's Entertainment Section. He is a graduate of Harvard Law School and currently lives in Los Angeles. He is the co-author, with Dina Appleton, of *Hollywood Dealmaking*.

LARRY ZERNER: Larry Zerner is a copyright, trademark, and entertainment attorney in Los Angeles who represents writers for both transactional and litigation matters. He can be reached at Larry@ZernerLaw.com.

The Editors

HOWARD MEIBACH: A leading expert in the spec script marketplace, Howard Meibach is the President of Hollywoodlitsales.com, Inc., an Internet company dedicated to helping writers and filmmakers connect with producers, agents, lawyers, and others in the Hollywood film community. Meibach is affiliated with Sony-based Escape Artists to find literary material and new talent on and off the Internet. Formerly, he worked in development with Ron Shusett, co-screenwriter and producer of *Total Recall* and *Alien*, and has also worked for Michael Jaffe, producer of dozens of network and cable television movies. Meibach is the writer of several screenplays and has authored a reference book for screenwriters, *Spec Screenplay Sales Directory*. He regularly lectures at writing seminars and classes throughout the United States and can be contacted through his Web site.

PAUL DURAN: Paul Duran is a writer-director of two independent feature films — *Flesh Suitcase* and *The Dogwalker*. His wide breadth of knowledge of the industry — in addition to screenwriting and directing, he has worked as an editor, art director, assistant cameraman, script reader, and journalist — has led Duran back to the classroom. He has lectured on independent filmmaking at USC and has taught screenwriting both here and abroad, most recently in Cuba. His next project, *Antarctica*, is currently in development.

ASK THE PROS

THE CRAFT

SCREENWRITERS

What makes a screenplay great?

DIANE DRAKE: Would that we could boil that down and bottle it. I'll say this though, when I was a development executive charged with the job of finding and recommending material that, as often as not, wasn't to my personal taste (i.e., horror pics, etc.), I remember thinking the scripts that struck me most strongly were the ones I really *felt*. The ones that somehow managed to inspire a genuine emotion: joy, sorrow, fear, laughter, whatever. And that, ultimately, is what I think people go to movies for — to *feel*.

CRAIG MOSS: Great story and great characters. What makes a great character involves great dialogue along with great action. Think of your favorite movies, then break them down some. Wasn't there a great story there? Weren't there great characters? Exactly.

CHARLES SHYER: It's a matter of taste, isn't it? For me, the two best screenplays ever are *All About Eve* and *The Apartment*. *Twentieth Century* is a close third.

ARNOLD SCHULMAN: Well, first, great writing. I think the problem now with screenplays is that they're all formulas that have been gotten from

Syd Field books and things that say, on page thirty-six you do this and on page forty-seven you do that. I'm not sure how much of that is because writers are treated with such disrespect or whether it's the other way around. But when I started in the business, you had to be established as a good writer, whether a novelist or playwright, before you got invited in to the industry. So the writing was appreciated. I remember my first picture — I was in my twenties, just a kid — Hal Wallace was producing the picture, George Cukor was directing, and Anna Magnani and Tony Quinn — they were big-time stars — were in it. Whenever anybody wanted to change a line, they would ask Cukor, "Can I say this instead of that?" and he would turn to me immediately and ask, "What do you think?" It wasn't in deference to me personally, it was in deference to the craft. I was hired because I knew my craft, and he knew his craft; we all respected each other. I think that made a huge difference in the quality of the writing.

DOUG WALLACE: I'd like to think it was the writing, but in a town that's driven by concept, and ever-hungry for fresh and commercial ideas, concept will usually win out. Unfortunately, a great concept doesn't necessarily mean a great screenplay, but it can at least get a check in your pocket and keep the ball rolling to the point where a great screenplay may come out of the concept. A great story with a great concept is hard to say no to. Add in great characters, great themes, great dialogue, great action, and a slight sense of style, and you'd be getting closer to the definition of a great screenplay.

DAVID GOYER: A great screenplay is one that makes you want to keep reading. One that sticks in your head long after you've finished; one that conjures up great imagery and characters, as opposed to great descriptions. There are a number of beautifully written scripts out there, in terms of their prose, that would not translate particularly well into great movies.

GREGG McBRIDE: Besides "Written by Gregg McBride" you mean? No, I'm kidding; honest!

I think that what makes a screenplay great goes beyond a terrific premise and even beyond expert storytelling. Sure, those are necessary ingredients no matter what the genre, but there have to be three-dimensional characters with heart in any type of script. Characters need to be cared about no matter what — and notice that I didn't use the word "liked." It's okay for a reader, or an eventual audience member, to not like a character, as long as he or she *cares* about following that character's story.

Another aspect that makes a screenplay great is really visual writing. Forget the fancy prose and well-crafted sentence construction. You want the reader — no matter what the level — to feel like they've just *seen* the movie when they're done reading your script. A great screenplay is very visual in the storytelling and leaves the reader visually stunned, elated, or intrigued.

JOHN FASANO: I think the main thing that makes a screenplay great is that it gets filmed! Seriously, I think the first key to a great screenplay is the main character. Your lead should not be a cliché or a cipher; he should be a real person. He should be a person the audience sees and thinks, "Damn, that could have been me." Even if the part calls for a super-brained scientist or superhuman cop, the things that make him accessible to the audience are the things that make him a great character.

Beyond that, I believe the best scripts ultimately have very simple plots, done elegantly. A big problem with a lot of scripts today is that their plots are so heavy on exposition and "reversals" that if any scenes don't make the final cut, the narrative falls apart. I am a strict believer in a film's logic being bulletproof, within the contexts of the internal logic. When I get notes from the studio or director that weaken the logic of the plot, I always work ten times harder to make those scenes work. You can imagine my frustration when the setup or payoff scenes fall on the cutting room floor, and then the reviews attack me for a sloppy script! As screenwriters, we are usually asked to write things we don't agree with — we have to make them work with us.

STEPHEN SUSCO: I'd have to say a fresh concept with a unique execution; believable, relatable and compelling characters; timeless stories with intelligent, non-clichéd dialogue; a message, subtext, or point-of-view carefully threaded through the spine of the story. And, from the viewpoint of a producer: enormous commercial potential.

ROBBIE FOX: Easy to read, fun, entertaining, not a homework assignment. A page-turner would be great, the shorter the better. People hate to read in Hollywood, worse than they did in high school — because they don't read for fun; they read to buy, and more often, they really just read to cover themselves, so if it sells elsewhere they can say they were on it. I read *Moby Dick* a few years ago, and it took forever, so I carried it with me for whenever I had some time to kill. Every time someone from the business saw my copy they would invariably ask, "Are you doing an adaptation of that, or...?" Reading for fun was otherwise inconceivable.

....

How do you come up with ideas?

C. Shyer: I have no idea how that process works. Thank God.

D. Goyer: Hmmm. God knows. Sometimes they come from my dreams. I got the job for *Dark City*, in part, because I had had a series of recurring nightmares as a child that corresponded with some of the imagery Alex Proyas was interested in exploring through his film. I am also a voracious reader. Frankly, I read more than I see films.

J. Fasano: I'm tempted to make some lame joke about having a box out in the garage filled with old *Tales from the Crypt* comics. Honestly though, I get ideas from *paying attention*. Wherever I go, whatever I'm doing, I'm aware of the things going on around me. I make connections between disparate images and ideas. In fact, while some people talk about how difficult it is to get an idea, I constantly find myself with ideas that I think would make great movies, but I just don't have the time to write — because I'm lucky enough to have paying gigs. It's a huge frustration because I'll be sitting in a diner listening to the waitress tell the story of how and why her son was beaten up on the way to the prom, and I tell myself I should write it down — but *Christine Refueled* or *Die Hard 5* is sitting in my Mac waiting for me when I get home.

D. Drake: I wish I knew — it would make it so much simpler the next time. I guess the closest thing I have to a "system," since primarily I write romantic comedy, is to try to think in terms of universal fantasies. What do I wish I could do? What does pretty much everyone wish they could do? And then try to take that basic kernel of desire and somehow make it possible, kicking it up in some way that makes it larger than life.

C. Moss: My partner and I sit in a room and try to think of concepts we would enjoy seeing as moviegoers. I might come up with something that doesn't quite work, but then he might build on it and come up with a better concept. Sometimes when we can't come up with anything — after many exhaustive hours of trying, we strip down and race through the streets of Santa Monica screaming, "Is it too late for Med School?!"

A. Schulman: I don't come up with an idea. I just start writing whatever comes into my mind, and then waste about two thousand pages before I see the beginning of a story coming along. It's completely non-cerebral. It just comes from wherever it comes from. It's not the most efficient way at all. I don't recommend it for anybody. But that happens to be the way I do it.

G. McBride: It seems like whenever I set out to think of ideas, they don't come. Or they're forced, which means they're not very good. Nothing's worse that pitching a bunch of one-liners to your managers and agents and watching their eyes glaze over. "Did you think of that on the way here in the car?" one agent asked me once. "No, on the way *to* the car," was my reply. Which wasn't exactly true, but hey, I was going with the flow.

> *I keep rewriting the same scenes over and over, and I can't seem to move on until I get them right. What should I do?*
>
> You should just move on. Even if you're unhappy. Don't let one scene paralyze you for the entire script. You can always come back to it. The screenplay is not finished yet. Often these scenes that we struggle with, fight over, and spend a week writing are the scenes that get cut from your final draft. They are giving you the most trouble because they have something inherently wrong about them. You may think you need it now, but later you'll discover that you don't. It's better to just work through it and get that first draft done. Once you get to the end, you can figure out the solution more clearly. If you need the scene, then maybe you can figure out a way of fixing it or combining it with another scene so that it makes sense.
>
> —*Larry Karaszewski*

All kidding aside, my best ideas happen out of the blue. I'll be in the car and just get "hit" with an idea. A germ of something that I'll then run by a few of my closest friends, who can be a tougher audience than my agents and managers. If they think there's something there, I'll craft the idea into a three-sentence logline and run it by my manager. She's great about telling me if I'm onto something or not. I've learned to not put too much into an idea before I do some checking. After all, you and Steven Spielberg may have gotten similar ideas at the same stoplight. And if he's already active on it, it doesn't warrant you getting active on it — unless, of course, you have a studio of your own.

But I also subscribe to the theory that there are no "bad" ideas and I keep everything in an overstuffed folder. What might not make a great feature this year might make a great TV pitch the following year — or vice versa. Germs of ideas are great places to start anything creative. Even if they come to you in the car.

R. Fox: I used to go out with girls, they'd turn me down, I'd write about it. Now I go out with my wife, get turned down, and I write about that.

J. Fasano: It's incredibly important for young writers to meet and interview people in all walks of life. How can you truly understand the characters in your piece if your only contact is with the kids you graduated from USC with? I started out as a journalist and interviewing, hell, just talking to everyone I meet is incredibly interesting to me, and all of their personality traits find their way into my writing. And I read a lot. I think all writers should read everything they can get their hands on, *especially* novels and historical books and magazines that are way out of their areas of interest. I've often found a fact in an obscure science magazine that made it into a plot or dialogue. I try to read a book a night, every night, and every magazine I can carry home from the newsstand.

D. Wallace: Ideas for me come in various ways: dreams, common everyday events, news, music, books, personal experiences; many things can

---

BUZZ WORD

Logline – A one-sentence description or summary of the storyline of a script, film, or TV program.

stimulate an idea. There is no magic formula, but sometimes there is a seeming magic.

Sometimes an idea just pops up from out of nowhere. Call it the collective unconscious, call it the muse, call it electrical patterns in the brain, but whatever you call it, the ideas are there for those on the lookout. For *Sevens*, a project I sold to Warner Bros. a few years back, the idea came to me from an image in a dream. That image so captivated my imagination that I begin to expand upon it until it ultimately led to me forming a story and writing the screenplay. For *Gargoyles,* a script that was bought by Paramount, that idea was very simply inspired by the gargoyles I've seen both in books and real places. How could fascinating and grotesque creatures such as gargoyles *not* make for an interesting story?

Philosophical questions have also inspired some of my work. Specifically, questions about memory and the nature of reality. These were ideas that I wanted to explore, and thus built a story around them in order satisfy my own longing for understanding. Alternately, sometimes it's a character type put in a peculiar situation that gets me excited.

But with all this said, I think it's more important that an idea excites you than understanding how it comes about. Any idea that excites you to the point of passion is the one you're going to write about.

· ·

How do you create characters?

R. Fox: The best characters, I think, are "captured" more than they are created. You observe real people in real situations, maybe combine them with other people you've observed, and then you can add in reasons they behave a certain way. Usually, the closer you stick to truth, the better chance you have of people saying, "Hey, I've been there."

C. Moss: I love studying people. So whenever I go out I take in everyone I meet. Some people stand out more than others, they have certain idiosyncrasies that just grab my attention — from there, I create a character.

D. Goyer: My characters tend to evolve through their actions. It depends on your point of view. I come from the Walter Hill/Clint Eastwood school, which means that a character is often what he or she *does*. Yes, you can slip into their subconscious and explore their relationships with their parents, but often, we *are* essentially what we *do*. I work from that central notion and build outward. For instance, Blade kills vampires. He is a machine. A weapon. And he is an effective weapon. I started from that notion. Then I tried to figure out how he would become that and what experiences would lead to the events depicted in those films. The rest grew naturally.

D. Drake: Once I have a sense of what the story is, and thus a vague notion of who these people, to some extent, have to be, then I think mainly in terms of dialogue. The things they say seem to tell me who they are. But you have to try to orchestrate them as best you can, and you can't just let 'em ramble for the sake of rambling — unless, of course, you're Quentin Tarantino.

J. Fasano: I take them from real people I've met in my life. I find the fit for the story I'm writing, and then take the character and his or her responses from a real person — that way the responses *feel* real. Too many scripts I've read over the last few years had characters drawn from other movies and TV shows.

C. Shyer: Hopefully, the inspiration for every character comes from some fragment of my life.

I've been told the lead character in my script needs more depth, more internal conflict, and that we need to care about him more. What are some strategies to fix this?

If someone is telling you these three things, they are probably telling you that they don't like your script. These are pretty major things. It sounds to me that the character is coming across as one dimensional. One shortcut would be to rethink how you are introducing the character. A lot of times, if you introduce someone in a different way, it colors everything that happens afterwards. If people are having trouble getting into your character, a Band-Aid solution would be to introduce the character with a little more conflict or sympathy because this introduction is going to shade how he or she is perceived throughout the rest of the picture. That's why when the studios do re-shoots, they usually re-shoot a new beginning or ending because those are the things that make the biggest impressions.

—*Larry Karaszewski*

R. Fox: Sometimes I write characters who are based on me, and people I'm close to, even my parents or grandmother, will say, "This guy is *not* likeable." Then I get depressed, because not only is my script no good, but I'm not even a nice guy. What I think they mean by that, though — unless I'm just completely kidding myself — is that my "script character" is not realized in a realistic enough way yet to overcome his weaknesses and flaws. This executive, Teddy Zee, once said to me, "No one is all anything. No one is all good, or all bad, people are complex; they may visit their grandmother more than all the other kids, but then they love hookers or something." I think I added the hooker part, but you get the idea.

G. McBride: I'll often base characters on people I know. Or assign them an identifying trait, usually something quirky, and go from there. Giving characters personality is very important to me, no matter what the genre is. And even little things can make a character stand out. I try to add depth to even my smallest characters, no matter how many lines they have in the script.

This is especially important when writing teen comedies, something I do a lot. You have a cast populated by thirteen- to seventeen-year-olds. How do you distinguish them from one another? I find the more personality, the better. For example, I recently had to create a "big sister" character who basically exists just to drive her little sister — one of the leads — around. I wondered, how can I make the big sister more interesting in such small snippets of time? That's when I came up with making her a devotee of Christian Rock — but with self-burned CDs that replace the name of Jesus with the name of her boyfriend. Just a cute little quirk, but one that makes the character memorable.

D. Wallace: I usually have an idea of who the main character is at the same time I come up with the basic concept. Since it's his journey, it's important to start learning about him as quickly as possible. I try not to be too academic in my approach to discovering the essence of my hero, but I do follow the age-old rule of discovering his objectives, both internal and external. This not only helps me to understand his character, but it also helps keep the story on track.

The antagonist and love interest usually come next in the process, and I define them in a similar way. But I always define objectives, even for supporting characters. I sometimes do biographical data and backstory, but try not to overdo it. I like to leave some room to discover who all these people are as I write. It's a cliché to say it, but the characters usually tell you who they are as you go along. That process never stops until the day you turn in the work.

A. Schulman: I really, truly, don't create characters. If I have seen somebody on the street and they pop into my mind, that's one thing, but generally, the characters create themselves. I just go along for the ride. I know that sounds pretentious, and I can't believe I said it, but that's what really happens. I don't have any preconceived ideas. The characters go wherever they want to go. Whenever I have had preconceived ideas, like, "he's going to wind up with her," it never happens that way.

. . . .

Do you write with specific actors in mind?

C. Shyer: Always...but they're usually dead.

D. Goyer: With the exceptions of the *Blade* films, I never write with a specific actor in mind. You never know who will ultimately be cast. Often, a script conceived as a vehicle for a female lead will be re-tooled for a male lead, and vice versa.

D. Drake: Occasionally. But I've never had the people I had in mind when I wrote it ever cast. Regardless, I find it can be helpful to have a certain type/voice in mind, as long as you don't get too boxed in by it — i.e. write a role that's so specific that only one bankable actor in Hollywood could possibly play it.

C. Moss: Absolutely; it helps give you a clear idea of who your characters are and at the same time it can help you sell your material.

L. Karaszewski: We think about a number of people who would be very good for it, but it's usually not very specific. When you're dealing with true stories, you tend to think of the real people. Our first script was written with two actors in mind. In the first draft we actually named the characters Albert Brooks and Morris Day.

A. Schulman: No, absolutely never, because I don't know who they're going to turn out to be. Even if an actor is already attached, I think it makes for a worse script because unconsciously, even though I try not to, part of my brain is recycling things I've seen the actor do before. That makes for lousy writing, as far as I'm concerned.

S. Susco: Sometimes — it helps me give each role a distinct voice, which is no easy task.

D. Wallace: It doesn't necessarily hurt to write for a specific actor, but it may not help either. Particularly if you don't get the actor you're hoping for. And at the development stage of the game, getting any actor involved is still a long way off. The better idea is to focus on writing the best and most believable characters you can. If focusing on a specific actor helps you do that, then all the better.

R. Fox: In my head, *So I Married an Axe Murderer* was always *Annie Hall*, if Annie just happened to be a murderer. Before I went off to write it — I sold it on a pitch — the studio executive at Columbia, Rob Fried, told me to write it for Woody Allen. Not that we would ever get him, but at the time, all the actors we envisioned for this movie were playing some form of that. Then, for an actual few weeks, Woody Allen actually wanted to be in the movie, no kidding. I was so excited, I had our first lunch together sixteen times in my head. "No, please, you're embarrassing me, Woodman...you really liked it?" Of course, that lunch never came to be. As it was told to me, he asked for seven million dollars, Columbia offered him five. They had a Mexican standoff for about two weeks, then he did *Scenes from a Mall* instead.

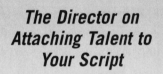

The Director on Attaching Talent to Your Script

"If a script comes with an actor attached, it certainly affects how you see the film. Hopefully it's the right actor. If it's the wrong actor, or if *you* don't think the actor is right for that specific piece, well, *then* you've got a problem."

—*Harold Becker*

J. Fasano: No. Unless they've been cast already, I write the character.

G. McBride: I often start out a script by casting the roles. I find it aids in an initial style of dialogue and character. But if I'm doing my job right and creating fresh, compelling characters, the actors I've "hired" for the roles I'm writing are usually "fired" halfway through the script and the characters become beings unto themselves.

....

What preparation do you go through before beginning a screenplay?

C. Moss: Lots of oiling up. Actually, we develop a detailed beat sheet/outline and then we're off and running.

G. McBride: It varies. But usually I think about it for weeks, even before beginning the notes or outlining process. Then one day, I start. A deadline always helps the start date. For specs, I try to create my own deadlines. I find the first thirty pages the most difficult to get through. There's something about knowing you need to fill 90-100 blank pages that can be kind of intimidating. Of course, working from an outline helps. But when you've created full and interesting characters, they can sometimes take you on a course you didn't originally set out for. Starting is easily the most difficult part of this job. But it's the biggest and most necessary step. That's for sure.

D. Wallace: First comes the idea. I usually jot it down as a note to myself, then let it germinate in my head for a while. Time passes and accompanying ideas join the original. At that point, I begin to map out the story into a rough synopsis. Once I've got a general idea of where it's going, I try to plug what I've got into some facsimile of the three-act structure. I also look at mythic structure to see how well my story falls into that order. Once that part is established, I plug in the characters, plot points, the themes, and as many visual treats as I can come up with. The rest I leave to discovery during the writing process.

D. Goyer: Before beginning a screenplay, I go into research mode. I have a full time assistant/researcher. But even before that, I spend an enormous amount of time doing research. Months, at least — it depends on the project. After the research, I start to beat out an outline. This is always the most painful aspect of writing, the nuts and bolts agonizing part where you have to figure out how Character A gets from Point B to Point C. Unfortunately, if you don't take the time to create that road map, you will ultimately lose your way when you go to script.

J. Fasano: I think. A lot. I read up on the subject I'm going to write about, and then I make notes, rough outlines, until I reach the point where I think I know what the film is going to be from beginning to end. That outline might be thirty pages long. I try to put every scene into it, even though there will be room for discovery. Then, only when I'm seeing scenes from the film in my sleep, do I sit down and write the script. By that point I'm just taking dictation from God and my own brain.

R. Fox: I generally write comedies, and with every comedy, there always seems to be a handful of movies that are the dramatic equivalents of that idea, so it helps to watch those with a pad in hand. It just gets you thinking in that world, so you can say, "Oh, if we just twist that a little, it'll be funny." I also like to travel to the city the movie takes place. Generally, studios will pay for this. If they do send you, you should get a T-shirt from wherever it is, and maybe even a snowglobe — studio people *love* snowglobes — and give them to the studio executive who approved the trip, along with a nice thank you note. This is proper etiquette, without it, the next writer might not get approved when he has to take his trip.

I once traveled with the band *KISS* for a week in the name of research. I took my grandmother across the country for a two-week trip. I even eloped with my sister-in-law one summer — all on Warner Bros. — each of them in the name of inspiration. Often my ideas come from an actual experience I had, so the experience becomes the preparation, only in retrospect. For this, one hopes to have taken good photographs to remind you of the trip, and ideally, receipts to remind the IRS of why you are — three years later — writing off a week in Hawaii as a business expense.

C. Shyer: Just a ton of notes and outlines; I'm nuts in this area. Anything to avoid staring at a blank page.

. . . .

Talk about your daily writing schedule.

D. Wallace: My schedule is to write all the time. I say that, essentially, because writing goes on even when you're not writing. If a story is strong enough to capture your imagination, then you should be thinking about it even when you're not at your desk.

But as far as a pragmatic schedule goes, I'm one of these perversely early risers who gets up at the most unholy of hours to work. I like the quietness and stillness of dawn. It's when I do my best work. The mind is fresh, ready, and everything seems possible. I usually start work between 4 and 6 A.M. and try to work about four hours before I take a real break.

After a bite of lunch, I'll come back and work another two to three hours in the afternoon. All of this is variable, of course, and dependent upon where I am with the work and what's on my schedule. When I'm close to finishing a piece, I often put in more time. I find that working every day keeps up the chops and makes the process slightly easier. I always work five days a week, sometimes seven. Of course, if you're on assignment, the faster you work, the quicker you can alleviate the stress of an impending deadline. This schedule works for me, but each individual has to find his own rhythm and timeline.

G. McBride: My friends think I'm insane. I'm up at 5 A.M. and I go work out. That way I'm home and in front of the computer by 7:30. I've already cleared out the cobwebs at the gym, but it's early enough that the phone's not ringing and the world is still fairly calm. I find mornings to be the best time to write — I can edit anytime of day. I try to use afternoons for meetings, phone calls, marketing, etc. Although if I'm under a deadline, the writing can happen at any hour of the day.

C. Moss: 10 A.M. to 6 P.M. I like having a regular schedule, just like most of the country.

C. Shyer: Every day, very disciplined. It's a job, mostly torture. Dorothy Parker had it right when she said, "I hate writing. I love having written."

J. Fasano: At 8 A.M. I drive over to Harlan Ellison's house and look through his garbage cans.

D. Drake: What schedule? After ten years at this, I still don't seem to really have one. When I'm going on something, I work day and night. When I'm not, I don't.

R. Fox: My work schedule experience is divided into two categories: before children and after children. Before children, I slept as late as my little heart desired, woke up fresh, made a few calls, took a swim, played some tennis, and then wrote into the wee hours of the morning — not for caffeine or bills, but for the sheer love of it and the need to express myself. Since children, I spend four or five awkward hours in bed with my wife, feeling rejected and claustrophobic, occasionally visited by a child who has had a bad dream or wet his bed. God forbid they sleep through the night, no doubt the stupid bird will have a bad dream and start squawking or the dog pisses in the house. So you wake up at like 6:00, and you go to Starbucks and you get this cup of coffee for three dollars and you have to treat it well, because you will refill that fucker all day long, until midnight and maybe later, so that after all the calls are made and the bills are paid, and you pick the kids up at school and you remember to go to your in-laws for dinner and your wife spends every fucking penny you have on crap you don't need, then, *and only then*, can you write for about eleven minutes. Until you get too tired and doze off at your desk.

A. Schulman: I don't have a schedule, actually. I don't seem to be able to do anything the way it's supposed to be done or the way other people do it. I write until I get tired and then I stop and take a nap. And when I'm writing, I don't read anything except a newspaper in the morning, and I don't go out; I just take one deep breath and stay there until a story emerges. And then I'll take a break, because now I know who the characters are, what it's about, and what the theme is. Then when I come back, I'm onto step two, a completely different phase. It becomes more like an adaptation then because I already have the ingredients.

D. Goyer: My writing schedule is very regimented. I write every weekday from 10:00 A.M. until 2:00 in the afternoon. I write in an office, away from home. Occasionally, I go away to a lodge in Wyoming to break the back of a first draft. I very rarely deviate from that schedule. Most effective writers have a self-imposed schedule; it's important to have structure, to treat this kind of creative endeavor as a "real" job, with a real schedule. I tried working out of home and found myself goofing off too much. I also write a *complete* first draft before I try to revise any individual part of the script.

J. Fasano: I try to keep a schedule based around when my kids have to be dropped off and picked up from school, so a typical weekday looks like this: get up 6 A.M., give my kids breakfast; 7:45 A.M., drive them to their various schools; 9 A.M., get back to the house in time to watch *Buffy the Vampire Slayer* reruns; 10 A.M., unlock the vault door to my office, write on and off until 2:30 P.M., pick up kids. All non-writing time I spend reading drafts, making mental notes, jotting things down on napkins and placemats and drawing in sketch pads. I like to draw out storyboards for certain scenes — I'll pin maps to the walls, I'll get props from the story and keep them on my desk so I can pick them up and remind myself what I'm writing about. Later, when the kids are asleep, I'll write some more. If I'm on a deadline, then all through the night.

L. Karaszewski: We both have kids, so we take them to school and allow the morning to start a little bit later. It's a 10:30 A.M. to 6:30 P.M. schedule. We treat it like a job and have an office outside our homes. Depending on what's going on, there tends to be a little procrastination — reading the trades, talking about what happened the night before, answering and returning phone calls — and then we start writing. We try to get a certain number of pages done a day, but we can only do so much. If we have a film in production, we're doing a rewrite, or someone's waiting for pages, then we can do an extraordinary amount of work in a short time.

S. Susco: On a good day: up at 6:00 A.M., coffee by 6:07, ten pages by 1:00. Work on the novel, or a short story, for another hour. Life outside the house the rest of the day.

On a typical day: up at 6:00 A.M., coffee by 6:07. Responding to email and surfing the 'net until 8:00. Gawking at the clock in disbelief until 8:02. Taking a much-needed break by 8:20. Going for a jog and watching a movie until noon. Thinking about lunch until 1:00. Getting lunch. Home by 2:30. Answering phone calls until 3:30. Putting on headphones and deciding to write straight through 5:30. Phone starts ringing off the hook at 3:45. On phone until 5:20. Taking a soak in the hot tub until

5:50. Turning off the phone to get some work done. Cell phone starts ringing. Phone calls until 7:00. Wonder what happened to the sun. Get out of the house. Back at 10:00. Pour a scotch, write until 11:30. Fall asleep.

•••

Which books on writing do you find most helpful?

D. Wallace: My advice to young writers coming up is to read everything you can. I've read many books on writing — most of the classics, and some not-so-classic. I've taken something from all of them. You never know when or where you might find a golden nugget, and it's certainly not going to hurt you in the meantime. But then there comes a time where you've pretty much read enough, and assimilation and application have to take over.

D. Goyer: I find very few writing books helpful. Honestly, I can't think of any.

C. Moss: Not to sound clichéd, but Robert McKee's *Story* helped me. Also *A Writer's Journey*. Both books were able to break down the screen writing process in ways that I could understand because I'm really not all that bright.

R. Fox: I like reading the autobiographies of great writers. I'm inspired by how they approach their work. I read Neil Simon's book, *Rewrites*, while I was on vacation in Napa Valley at some fancy resort. I remember reading about him sitting in some crappy six floor walk-up with a leaky skylight, and how it inspired *Barefoot in the Park*. Well, that certainly ruined my trip. How would I ever write something so great from Napa Valley? There are no walk-ups there. Comfortable lounge chairs and fancy umbrella-type drinks and lots of cheese, but no walk-ups.

S. Susco: The dictionary, *Story* by Robert McKee, *Hero With a Thousand Faces* by Joseph Campbell, the collected works of Shakespeare, my own diary.

C. Shyer: Reading good screenplays, watching good movies. Books about writing screenplays are usually written by people who can't write screenplays.

G. McBride: *Screenwriting 434* by Lew Hunter. *The Screenwriter's Bible* by Dave Trottier. And any screenplay you can get your hands on. Read! Read! Read!

R. Fox: Books on "how to write" I have no interest in. I know people go on and on about that Robert McKee guy, but I really believe he's had the most destructive influence on Hollywood since the beginning of film. I swear, every project, every batch of notes, people start quoting to you what page the inciting incident has to go on and at which point this character must be challenged by something from his past — you just know someone's been spending too much time analyzing the six subplots of *Casablanca*. It really makes no sense to me, this TV movie writer guy sees *Chinatown,* like, 500 times and suddenly everyone is changing the way they make movies. And it's not as if the movies are suddenly better. If anything, there's got to be less interesting stuff out there than ever before. I mean, as a rule, if you can put it into a formula, it's probably not very original, and isn't that the point?

J. Fasano: William Goldman's *Adventures in the Screen Trade*. That's it. All my other screenwriting reading has been the scripts to the films I loved growing up, to see how they got from the page to the screen. Screenwriting books may help others, but I think if you can write, and you understand that the story must have a beginning, middle, and end, just do it. Just get *Final Draft* so that it looks like a real script.

....

How many scripts did you write before you got paid?

C. Shyer: One.

C. Moss: Four.

D. Drake: Actually I was very lucky. I managed to sell my second screenplay and — miracle of miracles — it got made. But you have to bear in mind that before I finally got up my nerve to try to face the blank page, I had spent many grueling years in development, and had probably read hundreds of scripts.

S. Susco: Seven or eight.

D. Goyer: I wrote two scripts before I got paid. And they were stinkers. Most people's first few scripts are bad, that's just the honest truth.

J. Fasano: Ten. Fifteen.

D. Wallace: Two, or three before I got my first option. But then I sold three specs right in a row after that.

G. McBride: Too many to count. But it's all good. Each script was a labor of love. Even the bad ones.

R. Fox: I had been writing scripts since I was fifteen, five or six in all, including two three-act plays. Some time around my twenty-first birthday, I was working as a messenger for Embassy Pictures. I delivered a script to Arnold Schulman — one of Hollywood's true legends and a great, great writer, and he asked what I was working on. I told him, and he offered to read it. The next morning he called me and said, "Be at my house right after work for rewrites. If this thing doesn't sell, I'll turn in my Guild card." I showed up after work and watched him dictate *Chorus Line* dialogue in his robe as a hot secretary typed it all down scene by scene — this was the life! He ordered in enough Chinese food for 200 people and we got to work. Six weeks later he showed my script to his agent who said, "I'll have you fifty grand and an office on a lot within a month." A month later, Arnold left the agency and that agent stopped calling me back. He never did get me the fifty grand or the office, and that script never saw the light of day, though I had spent the money in my head ten times over. It took writing four more screenplays over the next two years before I optioned my very first script — for exactly $10,000 plus ten more for the rewrite. And I was thrilled to get it...though I *am* still waiting for Arnold's Guild card.

. . . .

How did you get your first paying gig?

C. Shyer: It was easy — nobody else was interested in writing a nurse's training film called *Introducing the Patient to His Room.*

G. McBride: I had big dreams about my first screenplay sale, the kind of dreams that spur young imaginations and motivate young minds. I would write *the* action blockbuster, one that would redefine stereotypical characters and scenarios. As I typed feverishly into my computer, I envisioned Jennifer Lopez or Linda Fiorentino uttering my words as the lead character — a cop transporting a dangerous criminal while being chased by the mob and dirty cops through an earthquake-ravaged city.

Little did I know that the B-movie company that bought the script would have other ideas. No big writer's fee. No big stars. The lead would go to Traci Lords (billing herself as the extra-fancy Traci *Elizabeth* Lords) and the male lead would go to Gary Daniels. "Who?" I asked the producers. They were very excited, informing me that he's an international kickboxing champion. "That's great," I thought, "given that his character is a *banker.*" Still, it was the best feeling in the world. My script was being bought. And the good news about the B-movie company was that they bought scripts to actually make movies, not "develop" them.

C. Moss: As a stripper or...? Oh, as a writer. It was a spec sale. Our manager sent it out to various places and we got very lucky and someone bought it.

D. Goyer: Just out of film school I sold a script called *Dusted,* which ultimately became the Van Damme picture *Death Warrant.* It went immediately into production and I got to hang out on set. While it wasn't a very good film, at twenty-one years old, it was an amazing experience. Ever since then, I've been able to support myself as a screenwriter.

D. Drake: I was working in development as the VP of Creative Affairs for Director-Producer Sydney Pollack. He's a great guy, but in my heart I knew I couldn't keep up the development grind much longer, and I wrote my first script at night. It didn't sell, but it did get me an agent at a small agency; with [Pollack's] help I was able to land a scale writing assignment to do a treatment. At that time, a feature treatment paid about $25,000, and as my overhead was meager, that money (coupled with the unemployment insurance that followed), bought me the time it took me to write my second script, *Only You*, which, saints be praised, sold big.

J. Fasano: I was painting the one-sheets — movie posters — for a low budget film company in Manhattan called Reeltime. They were making a sorority slasher film called *Blood Sisters* and the script was just awful — they had the guys from the mental institution with butterfly nets, for Christ's sake! I said I could re-write the script for them because I had studied writing and film in college, and so I did a pass — uncredited, welcome to the world of the screenwriter — and they shot the film. Another producer, Jack Bravman, heard about what I did for Reeltime and asked me to write and direct the film *Zombie Nightmare* in Montreal for $5,000. I did, and ended up without either a writer *or* a director credit for the sake of the Canadian tax shelter. Do I see a pattern developing here? Anyway, the film ended up starring a young Tia Carrere and an old Adam West and was subsequently on *Mystery Science Theatre 2000* where I was *glad* my credit was only "assistant director."

D. Wallace: My first paying gig was while I was still in film school at UCLA. A fellow student, who already owned his own commercial production company, wanted to make a film about the experiences of a young immigrant woman he knew. He paid me five hundred dollars to do a story treatment for him. That was the first money I got for writing, and that just sort of fell into my lap.

My first industry gig came from my work finding its way into the hands of a TV producer. My first agent — who really wasn't that great an agent, but did get one of my early screenplays optioned — used that script to get me the work. Though I was still a non-union writer at the time, he parlayed my writing sample into a submission at Laurel Entertainment, who were producing *Monsters* and *Tales From the Darkside*. They loved the writing and the subject matter, and ultimately gave me the gig.

BUZZ WORD

Ankle – A classic (and enduring) *Variety* term meaning to quit or be dismissed from a job, without necessarily specifying which; instead, it suggests walking: "Alan Smithee has ankled his post as production prexy at U."

R. Fox: I had a friend at Northwestern who used to try to help me study when I was on academic probation, but I was always sleeping, so it was hard to actually be an effective student. Then I quit Northwestern — and NYU and UCLA shortly thereafter, for good measure. A few years later I'm working as a messenger at Embassy Pictures and the same girl moves to Hollywood and needs a job. So I help her get one as a receptionist at Embassy. Three years later she's working for a producer and actually buys my script. In the years after that, she produces *Speed* and *Saving Private Ryan*. Lesson: You can sleep and you can quit college, but while you're awake, be nice to everyone — you never know.

. . . .

Do you prefer to write on spec or on assignment? Why?

L. Karaszewski: Right now, we're writing our first spec since *Ed Wood*. We've been very blessed in that we've been able to have a career that includes a large number of eccentric choices that, fortunately for us, got made through the studio system. Sometimes you have to do something for yourself, and that's where the spec script comes in. You can do it exactly the way you want to with no interference. We haven't felt that we sold our souls because we're writing crazy movies like *The People vs. Larry Flynt*. It's interesting writing on spec again. It's nice to have no one to please except yourself. The problem is that most people who write specs are trying to make some big sale and they end up compromising. We write a spec to clear our heads. *Ed Wood* came about because we were trapped in crappy kiddie comedy-land. The *Problem Child* films were very successful but they were a style of filmmaking that we were not that interested in continuing. But when we went in and pitched more serious projects, people would laugh at us saying, "You're the guys who wrote *Problem Child*!" We were told we weren't good enough to write our own ideas. That kind of thing freaked me out. So in a sense, we wrote *Ed Wood* as a spec in order to do something that we weren't being allowed to do in the studio system. That film made our name as writers.

G. McBride: Spec is fun because you're writing the script with your total vision. On assignment is fun because you're being *paid* to write. As a writer, I think it's always important to have many balls in the air. Which means if you're lucky enough to be writing something on assignment, then you should be working on your own spec at the same time. This also provides relief from the notes process, since no one's giving you notes on your spec. At least not until you show your agents and managers, that is.

J. Fasano: I prefer to work on assignment because I want to know what the end of the game is going to be. In many cases an assignment already has elements attached to it, so you're not floating out at sea — money has been spent and that gives the project a forward momentum. You can feel the difference when people want to get the film made; it imbues all your actions with "purpose." As for spec scripts giving you more creative freedom, well, once you sell it, a spec becomes an assignment, doesn't it? And now you're in a position of getting notes and fighting and making compromises — if you're lucky. My first Hollywood sale was a spec script; it got me started, but it never got made. That's the thing I hate the most — the development deal that will never get made. Yeah, you get paid — usually more than the ones that do get made — but it's masturbation — a lot of sweating and grunting that produces no issue.

Adapting a Play to the Screen

"When I adapted my own play, *A Hole in the Head*, there were no film schools and there weren't any books on how to write a film. I just went to a lot of movies and studied them, and realized — and this is not an original thought now, but it was original to me then — that movies are written in a different language than prose. It's a visual language and completely different. Hal Wallis, who was one of the most important producers in the business back then, told me about the time he hired S.M. Berman, who was one of the most famous playwrights, to write a movie for him. In the first scene, he had to dramatize that a husband had lost interest in his wife. He wrote fifteen pages of absolutely brilliant dialogue which Hal said would be great for a play, 'But here's how we do it in the movies. A man and his wife walk into the elevator. He's wearing a hat. They go down a floor, the doors open, in comes a beautiful woman. He takes off the hat.' That told me everything I needed to know about how to write movies. It related to everything that I think has to do with movies. If you can do it in one shot visually, do it. It's a visual medium. I regret that because I love dialogue, but that's what it is."

—Arnold Schulman

D. Drake: Spec, spec, spec. It's a very risky way to try make a living, but what in this business isn't? I feel like we, as screenwriters, have so little control and say over what we create — at least let me keep that initial draft. I really don't know how people who work on assignment do it, what with all the different players wanting their viewpoint incorporated. You have to be much more adept at both marketing and politicking than I apparently am. My hat is off to them.

D. Goyer: I have no preference for writing on spec or assignment. As a more established writer, I don't really have to write on spec anymore. But it's nice, from time to time, to just write something without any outside involvement or consideration. I'm lucky in that the types of things I enjoy writing about seem to be fairly popular with the studio.

C. Moss: Assignment. Because then you know you're getting paid for the hours you're putting into it. A spec can be liberating because you're writing what you want, but in the end there's the chance it might not sell. And who in their right mind wants that? Right? Right?

C. Shyer: Now, usually on assignment. I like getting paid.

R. Fox: The advantage of selling up front is obvious: You get the money, and even if you go into a coma they can't take it away from you. Also, you don't spend five months writing something and then — ten minutes before you type "Fade Out" — you see the same stupid premise show up on the side of some bus starring Ben Stiller. But I much prefer the process of writing on spec. There's something heroic about it. "Look at me, I don't care about money, about jobs! I have a story to tell and nothing will get in the way of telling it!" No one tells you you're taking too long — no one tells you anything, really. They just say, "Oh, it sounds good, I'd love to see it when you're done." People do get pretty excited about new spec scripts. You can make a lot of friends by telling a producer "I want to include you in my spec script auction." And then you piss a lot of people off when you don't let them read it first, because they all feel like, "Hey, I gave you your big break." Yeah right, since when is not returning someone's call for six months a big break? The truth is, we are in a business where you can turn paper into gold. It happens all the time, just look in *Variety*. So you call everyone who has been begging you for a sneak peek of your new masterpiece over the past five months, and you put it out there. But if it doesn't sell within a day, it'll probably never sell. Then you have this giant gap in your work life and a whole bunch of bills to catch up on.

S. Susco: Both. I usually have three projects going at the same time: a "food on the plate" assignment; a project I'm trying to set up; and a spec. Working on multiple projects at the same time keeps any one of them from getting old.

D. Wallace: I'm a spec kind of guy. I like to write my own stuff, specifically because I'm more in love with my own ideas than those of my fellow man. Not that I can't appreciate the ideas of others, but to write at all takes so much time and work — to do anything but your own stuff just seems the less satisfying way to go.

Additionally, to write something you don't feel passionate about — as in rewriting somebody else's work — can become not only laborious, but also tedious. Of course, as I say that, I realize I could use one of those tedious jobs right about now, just for the paycheck.

But given the best of all possible worlds, I prefer to develop my own ideas. With that said, one should not lose sight of the fact that every spec, no matter how well-written, is a crapshoot. The industry is fickle and the marketplace ever-changing. Movies are expensive and great risks must be undertaken. In retrospect, I realize I could have written and published half a dozen books over the years, instead of all the specs I've written that the studios didn't buy.

....

Have you ever written with a partner? What are the advantages or disadvantages to writing solo?

C. Shyer: I've always written with a partner — too lonely without one.

A. Schulman: No. I've never even tried. It would be unthinkable to me. I've been writing since I was ten years old, and it's a very pleasantly solitary thing for me.

C. Moss: I have a partner. However, we work in a very unorthodox manner. He's into missionary and I'm more into straight doggy, so we're very different. To be honest, I like working with a partner, especially because we write comedy and it's good to bounce things off each other. It's good synergy, if you will, though I have no idea what synergy means. However, by writing solo you get to keep all the money. Yeah, I didn't think about that. Interesting....

D. Wallace: Never had a writing partner. I'm of the mind that the best art comes from the original vision of one artist. Of course in the film business, no movie — or I should say very few movies — reach the screen without having myriad fingerprints on them.

D. Goyer: I have only written with a partner once. It didn't turn out particularly well. I like writing alone. I think it's an individual decision. Some people work well with others, batting ideas back and forth, etc. But I have developed a very individual style of working that wouldn't mesh, I'm sure. I have a kind of shorthand when I am researching, beating out a story, and so on.

L. Karaszewski: You have to realize that killing each other isn't necessarily a negative. Battles over content are not personal battles. The arguing can lead to good work. We write everything in a room together. Scott [writing partner Scott Alexander] is the typist and sits behind the computer. I pace back and forth or lie on the couch and throw out ideas. I started by writing sketch comedy in which everything is done in a room with a group. When I'm asked how we write, I always refer to the old *Dick Van Dyke Show*. Morey Amsterdam, Rose Marie, and Dick Van Dyke were all in a room coming up with ideas and one person sat behind a typewriter. Some writing teams say, "You take that scene and I'll take this scene," or, "You take the first act and I'll take the second act." That's really individual writing stitched together. Scott and I co-write everything.

J. Fasano: I have never written with a partner in terms of the two of us "Cash & Epps"-style, sitting in the same room with one computer, with each taking the next two lines. Even when partnered with other writers, including my wife, we have worked separately — each on a whole draft at a time, and then talked about it. Writing for me is a solitary process, but by the time I sit in front of the keyboard I know what ideas I want to put down. A large part of my writing process is thinking and pre-planning, and I just do that better alone.

R. Fox: The disadvantage of writing with a partner is — obviously — you have to share the money. That really stinks. Especially if you're used to writing alone. It pisses you off enough when you get a check and your agent has already subtracted his 10 percent. If you have a manager, he's subtracted *his* 10 percent, too. So if, on top of that, some bastard is taking 50 fucking percent for sitting on your couch and eating donuts while *you're* the goddamn genius, then that sucks. In any case, I write alone. But I did once have the good fortune to write a TV show with my college roommate, Billy Ray (*Hart's War, Shattered Glass, Volcano*). We wrote a TV show about two college roommates and based it on all our experiences together at Northwestern. But the network made us change it to roommates five years *after* college, to increase our audience, or so they said. Unfortunately, we didn't have any experiences to draw from about being roommates five years later, so maybe that's why it never went to series.

G. McBride: I have never written with a partner. I think of writing partners like I think of roommates. I better be getting some really good sex to put up with the stressful stuff. Thus, I write alone. But I love it. And there are always agents, managers, and producers around who like to *think* they're your writing partners.

S. Susco: I have, twice. Writing with a partner can be a great experience. It challenges you to break out of your own habits, many of which may be

> ### *The Director on Working with the Writer*
>
> "I like to work closely with the writer. I believe in that process. And certainly I'm going to have some input, depending on the script, so it becomes, in a sense, a joint commission. I have to see how to turn it into a film. We talk about it, I'll read the script carefully over and over, maybe I'll have a reading with some actors, I may do some editing — all of these things are involved. Then I'll come to some conclusions about what I feel needs to done. I've rarely come across what you can call a perfect script, ready to go. But then I let the writer do his job — *write*."
>
> *—Harold Becker*

45

bad ones; working with a partner can also force you to try something new. But a partnership is like a marriage, one that, in most cases, is in need of constant therapy. Open dialogue and understanding is the key. But writing solo — even on the side, while working in a partnership — builds a kind of self-determination, free of any reliance upon others, which is invaluable for a roller-coaster career in screenwriting.

D. Wallace: There are those who subscribe to the philosophy that two heads are better than one. In some cases, I'm sure that's true, particularly in the rewriting process. A new head offers an objectivity that the solo artist just can't get when he's in the midst of writing a piece. So in that sense, a partner can be an advantage. But on the other hand, he can also be a detriment. Sometimes a story can get steered in the wrong direction by a second party. Confusion may ensue and the writer may lose track of his original vision. I personally feel the disadvantages outweigh the advantages. I believe the writer has to listen to his own heart and mind. Even if the answers don't come immediately, if one is determined, they will come. And most likely they'll be better than the ones you'll be getting from the other guy.

J. Fasano: The only time I sit in straight collaboration is when the director has been hired and we're doing drafts that are headed for production. Then I like him sitting right next to me while I type. I don't want to finish a whole draft, hand it to him and have him say, "No, that's not what I meant." I want to be able to write an exchange, ask, "Like that?" and get an immediate response. I learned this after years of having directors (big, powerful directors who shall remain nameless) change their minds after I handed in a draft. Now, if we are in active pre-production, that sucker is sitting right next to me while I do my rewrite. Believe me, at that point, it allows me to cut the process in half. No surprises.

D. Drake: I've written with a partner twice. First time — but for the niggling fact that we ultimately did not manage to sell the script — was a really good experience. We were both on the same page, literally and figuratively, equally committed and desirous of seeing it happen. And we had fun.

The second time, with the exact same partner, was an absolute and utter nightmare, a little circle of hell that I hope to never revisit. Suffice to say, you have to be extremely careful to choose someone who is, at the *minimum*, as committed to the enterprise as you are. Ideally more. You want someone in the same place at the same time in terms of willingness to put in the time, energy, and hard work or you'll wind up wasting your *own* precious time, energy, ideas, and sanity — *and* they'll still expect 50 percent of the proceeds. Personally, I don't think I will *ever* do it again. As a friend who had worked with a partner advised me many, many, moons ago when I was just starting out, "if you can do it on your own, do it on your own." I wish I'd had that advice tattooed behind my eyeballs.

. . . .

Does the writer need to be thinking about budget and/or marketplace when writing a spec script?

J. Fasano: This is tough. You can think about market so much you fool yourself into thinking you have a slam dunk on premise when the script is too weak to sell. Ultimately, I think the writer should sit down and write whatever the hell he wants. Look at it this way, if you write something you've tailored to what you think is the market and it doesn't sell, you feel like you wasted a half a year. But if you wrote a great script on what you wanted, and no one bought it, at least you're proud of it — and maybe you can sell it later, or adapt it for television, or even make it yourself on DV or something.

As for budgets, I directed my first 35mm feature film on a $52,000 budget, and have written projects that cost almost one hundred million. The cost of the movie is the level of elements. First find a really great story you want to tell. Tell it right and you will get something out of it.

C. Shyer: Short answer: Yes.

C. Moss: Absolutely. That's what executives are looking at. Have a clear idea of who you're writing this movie for and generally what the budgets are on previous movies in that genre.

G. McBride: Only if writing on assignment with the supervision of a producer or studio that knows what their limitations are. But I've found that even with this in mind, everyone knows it's about making the script as

If I'm going in to pitch a project, how do I prepare?

In the early days before we were well known, Scott and I treated pitching like a performance. We rehearsed everything. We had another screenwriter, Daniel Waters, who wrote *Heathers* and *Batman Returns*, pretend to be the studio executive and we would pitch him an idea. This was before any of us had actually sold anything. Dan would purposely try to trip us up. He would ask us if we wanted a soda in the middle of a thought or deliberately misunderstand something. These pitch rehearsals trained us for action. Another secret is to try to keep the pitches as short as possible. Also, let them know that the pitch is beginning. We like to give them a thirty second overview about what the movie is before we get started. We feel it's important to tell them where they are in terms of the story. We announce that this is what's happening on page thirty, or at the end of Act Two the father dies, so they get a sense of the pace of the story. Because the bottom line is that if you've given them those markers, it's going to help them retell the story to their bosses.

—Larry Karaszewski

good as possible more than it is about keeping it under a certain budget. That comes later. First comes the ever-elusive greenlight.

R. Fox: People write specs for one of two reasons. First, you think you have a killer idea that's very commercial, very high-concept, and very castable — but if you were to sell it on a picth, you'd just get your price, whereas on the open market you just might bring down the house. In this instance, yes, keep the script as short as you possibly can, polish and punch it with every bit of talent you can muster, and without a doubt keep in mind things like, "Is it too expensive?" "Why would an actor star in this movie?" and, "Is it commercial?"

The other reason for writing on spec is when you have a great idea that you *know* has no way of selling on a pitch, but it's in your heart too much to ignore it. So you decide that if you're true to the material and the inspiration, it'll possibly find its way into someone else's heart, too. For this second plan, maybe the most important part is that you write it from the same place it originated: in your heart. Don't worry about the other crap, budget and casting — because you've already made the deal with yourself that as long as you're happy with it, you'll be glad you did it. I was very lucky to have as a mentor and director the great Herbert Ross, and he always said, "If you work hard on something you love, then the work will be the reward itself."

In any case, the worst thing to do is sell out on your passion project — because when it doesn't sell, then you really feel like an idiot. And who knows, maybe it will sell, or maybe it's the script you had to get out of your system to get to your next script that *will* sell. I'm a huge Woody Allen fan and I really hated *Interiors*, Actually, I don't believe I ever made it all the way through *Interiors*, but I'm sure I would have hated it. However, for some reason, I believe that he had to make that film to get from *Annie Hall* to *Manhattan*, so for that I appreciate him doing it.

D. Wallace: Not specifically, but it's a good idea to be aware of the marketplace you're writing for, and how your project fits into the budgetary scheme of things. Tentpole scripts garner a lot of attention but they also create fear in readers and studio execs. Stories with big action sequences and special effects, although exciting to conjure and see played out in the finished product, can also cause a script to be more easily shot down. Everybody is afraid in Hollywood, and seeing a 100 million dollar budget may tickle their fancy, but it also sends up a red flag. This should only be a tool, not a rule. Bottom line: Write whatever gets you going, just be aware of the pros and cons of all your choices.

D. Goyer: I don't advise beginning writers to think about marketplace. Or even budget. If you try to time the market, by the time your film gets bought or made, the audiences will be on to something new. Although, as far as budget goes, if you are interested in directing your script, then cheaper is better. But beyond that, you should just write about what inspires you. What you think is funny, scary, touching, etc.

S. Susco: Yes and no. A smart writer is aware of the market limitations they're building into a script. And if a writer is looking to write a huge blockbuster and make a million-dollar sale, then they must be especially

---

BUZZ WORD

Tentpole release – A film that the studios expect to open hugely; usually a summer release and often an action film, tentpole releases are generally the beginning or continuation of what is hoped to be a successful franchise.

focused on this. But if a writer is writing something more personal, from the heart, I always advise that they don't give a flying fuck what anyone has to say. Write your damn heart out. If it's a good story, someone will buy it.

. . . .

Can you discuss the relationship between screenwriter and producer; when do fight and when do you give in?

G. McBride: I come from the world of advertising, which was a great place to learn that nothing is created in a vacuum. There are always going to be other people's opinions. And many of those people are more powerful than you are and they *will* get their way — with or without you. Thus, I make sure to keep the discussion flowing at all times. If I don't agree with a note I will fight it, by explaining why my way makes sense for the project. Usually the producer will listen and then agree to "try it." But this can also be Hollywood-speak for, "I'll just get the writer we hire after you're gone to do it my way, anyway."

C. Moss: You have to learn how to pick your battles carefully. Give up the small stuff in exchange for the stuff you're most passionate about.

J. Fasano: I look at the issue in this way: if I'm sitting home writing a spec, it's mine completely. When I attach a producer, it's ours — a partnership. If it's bought outright, the balance of power shifts to the producer even more, and when a director is hired, I answer to him. As to when to fight, it's simple — when you feel that it will destroy the film not to fight; or when it's more important to have your vision remain intact than it is to see the film made.

In studio development deals it's quite a different animal. If you fight, you will be replaced. Period. In fact, if you *don't* fight you'll still be replaced eventually. Sometimes I have fought and been bounced and was sad over it for years; other times I've done everything the producer asked, bent over backwards, and still been replaced with the "flavor of the month." So you can fight when you want, but if you, yourself, are not the producer or director, in the long run it will be out of your hands.

D. Wallace: This varies, of course, depending on who the producers are, the type of project, and how they like to work. But most — at least most of the producers that I've come across — always want to get more out of you than they are willing to pay for. It's an old industry game, and a bad one. It's called, "Let's try to get the writer to write for free."

Unfortunate as that is, not all writing experiences run that course. The best experience I've had was in working with some producers over at Warner Bros. In our early meetings, I told them what I wanted to do, and they — seeming to like my ideas — sent me off to write. When I turned the work in some weeks later, they were happy and didn't even ask for a second run-through, which I was contractually obligated to do. After all the horror stories I'd heard about rewriting, I was amazed that my situation worked out so amicably.

But believe me, that was an anomaly rather than the norm. Most of my other writing projects have involved fierce battles over both context and content. This is not to say that all producers are evil, though some certainly are, but generally speaking, there always seems to be a lack of consensus between the producers, the studio, and the writer.

To be too belligerent in this battle for power is a death wish. You have to bend, but you have to also know when not to. To keep working, choose your battles wisely. Some ideas are worth fighting for, some may

The Director on Writers on the Set

"If I had my druthers, I'd have the writer with me all the time — but writers usually have other commitments, other things they're writing, and they're not getting paid to be on the set. But if the writer is willing to be on the set with me, I'm happy to have him there. I've had writers with me for good parts of the time. It's an ongoing process because things are always happening during the shooting. Certainly I always have the writer with me through rehearsals, and since I'm into long rehearsal periods before I start shooting, it's a good time for the writer, the actors, and myself to come together on the script. There's a lot give and take — hopefully not a lot of rewriting, but there's always some tweaking. Sometimes you see something doesn't work, so you have to go at it again. I think that's a process that the writer enjoys, and it's one that I love."

—Harold Becker

not be. The best working relationships are give and take, but again, it becomes a matter of how much do you give and how much will you take. One of the projects I worked on, which I won't name here, had six producers and three development people involved. You don't have to be in the movie business to see a recipe for disaster there. Nobody could agree on anything. And when they finally did agree upon something, a week later it would change. I was the first in a long line of writers on that project. Four years later it *still* hasn't been made.

G. McBride: While I try not to be a whore and accept every note just to keep working, I do try to remember that these people are paying me. Even with this philosophy, I have seen producers ruin projects, usually when there are way too many of them and all of them have ideas of their own. But I've also seen my work get stronger. And at the end of the day, if I have the writing credit, that benefits me. I think it's important for any writer to remember that it's not about artistic integrity as much as it's about getting your work sold and, more importantly, getting your work *made*. The notes process is going to happen. Might as well be with you instead of without you.

C. Moss: There are two types of producers — smart ones and dumb ones. If they're smart, meaning they have knowledge of storytelling and screenplay structure, then you tend to get a lot out of them — they have good ideas, they're good sounding boards, etc. But if you get paired up with a dumb producer, you're in for a *loooong* ride.

R. Fox: Give in on everything you don't really care about, and fight for everything you really believe in. Bottom line: It won't matter anyway, unless you have an Oscar or are the director. It's not a democracy. They write the notes, you do them.

C. Shyer: Always fight. Never give in.

S. Susco: This is, in my opinion, largely dependent upon the writer's ability to walk away from a job if need be. It's a case of picking one's battles. Be deliberate and decisive about what you choose to stand firm on. But at all times, a writer should argue and fight for their ideas, and against those ideas they feel are dishonest to the story. If a writer chooses not to do that, and keeps his mouth shut, then he's not doing his job — and he's failing the producer who hired him, too. It is a writer's job to speak up, but also to understand that the "boss" is, in most cases, the final arbiter of "all things creative." So it is the writer's job to win the producer over to the creative side, while still being open to being convinced otherwise.

G. McBride: One trick I've learned is that when someone gives a note, you don't have to realize it *fully*. By just ushering in the "idea" of the note into the script, the producer is often satisfied that he or she has been heard. Then everyone feels like they've contributed and everyone feels more attached to the script.

A. Schulman: Most times, with few exceptions, I've had wonderful experiences with producers because I made it clear before we started that I was an equal player. Even though I may have been a writer-for-hire, I was going to give them more than they wanted, and therefore I also expected more than they wanted to give me. We were in this as equals or I wasn't going to do it. And if they said, "Yes," but didn't do it, I quit. Still, there were a few cases where they just disregarded me entirely. When I spoke at UCLA or somewhere recently, all they wanted to know was how you *steal* credit. My problem has always been the opposite — how to get my name *off* the script because it had been screwed it up so badly. I don't want to name any names, but just look at the pictures. You'll see the ones that are really, really dogs.

....

What's the worst note you ever received on one of your screenplays?

S. Susco: "Does it have to be a boar?"

C. Moss: The worst note: "Can you have the character say, 'Yep,' instead of, 'Yeah'?"

D. Goyer: I was once told to make a script 20 percent funnier. Why not 30 percent? Hell, why not a 100 percent? The alarming thing is that, sometimes a person will be giving you notes and it's clear that they haven't really read your script, or they're simply reading the coverage. It's disheartening, especially after having spent so much time trying to craft a good read.

J. Fasano: After fifteen years? There have been so many that I'm writing a book! But one good one was the exec who couldn't understand why the lead woman would wait years for the return of her fiancé. When I said, "Because she loves him," he said, 'Nah, there has to be a *reason* — like he knows where there's a secret formula or something." I swear, this is verbatim!

G. McBride: This is the honest-to-God truth: For a family movie I was writing, I got this note: "I think maybe the third act needs some aliens." I balked and told the producer I was going to tell everyone he suggested that. He laughed...then said, "Really, I'd like to see aliens worked in." So I did it.
  And they got cut during the next go-round!

R. Fox: It's not about the worst note, it's that I followed so many of them. I mean, you have to listen, but you have to be careful not to listen *too* well. Use your own creative instincts to figure out what they're missing, but don't necessarily use their answers to solve the problem. I once spent years working on a play, and while contractually I didn't have to listen to anyone as the author — you partner with good people, they have ideas, at the time they sound workable, at the time they may even sound great, but you have to be careful about making last-second changes. I can remember changes I made to certain scenes that now make me cringe, but at the time I was saying to myself, "What an amazing idea, why didn't I think of that?"

C. Shyer: We were asked to make Judy Benjamin — the Jewish American Princess in *Private Benjamin* — from Texas instead of Philadelphia.

D. Wallace: I honestly can't remember a worst note. I mean I've had some critiques that haven't set well with me, but something that stood out as being absolutely horrible...I don't remember ever receiving one of those. I've been heartbroken when told a story isn't really working, but usually there's some thought there that is constructive and generally inspires me to get back into the work and do a better job. Everything can be improved, and you should be open to doing that. But then again, your critics aren't always right either. It's good to develop a built-in stink detector and arm yourself with it. That takes time to perfect, but ultimately, it's your best aid in evaluating what you've created.

....

Do you have an agent, manager or both? What are the advantages of having both?

J. Fasano: In the old days I had an agent who acted like he was also my manager. We talked about career goals, and how a particular project fit in them. He was both agent and father confessor. But he retired. Now I have many agents at ICM, and one manager, Craig Baumgarten. The main reason I have both is that there are so many people out there who are looking for the same jobs I am that just one individual can't keep track of them. I have an agent for long-form TV who's brilliant, an equally adept TV series agent, two feature agents, and my manager. I would say that my work comes equally from all of them. Now, with an attorney, that means I am paying commissions of 25 percent off the top of my income, but the goal is to work, and without my team I would not have worked as much as I have the last ten years.

D. Wallace: I've had both, but not at the same time. My first manager I took on several years ago. But to be honest, I wasn't blown away by the relationship, or what came out of it. In theory, managers are supposed to give you a lot more hands-on attention. In reality, I don't think that's necessarily true. As a writer, a manager usually has more to gain from you than you do from him. He's often also a producer, or a wannabe producer, and at best a dubious advocate with more mixed motives than an agent will generally have.

I've had bad agents, too — agents who could barely pick up the phone — but I've also had good agents who worked with me noun by pronoun to shape a project and then busted their asses to sell it. Unless you're having tremendous success and need a lot of extra care, one agent or one manager at a time is plenty. And why pay out an extra 10 percent when it's hard enough to get one representative to do what you want and need, much less two? If your agent or manager is a good salesman, that's a plus, but what may be more relevant — i.e., the essential and most important element of the writer/agent relationship — is that you get somebody who likes and appreciates the type of work you're doing. Passion counts for a lot. An agent whose sensibilities lean toward romantic comedy will, generally speaking, not be a good agent to rep your sci-fi script. Of course, if you're just starting out, any agent who responds to your work will do. Later on, you can afford to be a little more picky.

C. Shyer: Not sure either is an advantage. Pretty certain the latter is redundant.

C. Moss: [My partner and I] have a manager. My belief is go with whomever is supporting you and getting you work. I see no reason to have both. You're throwing away 10 percent! That's just not healthy.

D. Goyer: I have an agent. I briefly had a manager, but that was an odd situation. My first agent stopped agenting and decided to go into management. I tried it for a while, but it didn't really work for me. I tend to be a self-starter, and I don't discuss my ideas with my agent before writing, so I don't need any additional handholding. I suppose some people need that, and for them, it might work. But I honestly can't see the reason to be paying two commissions for what essentially amounts to the same type of work. Ideally you don't *need* both. Not if an agent or manager is really doing his or her job. The job descriptions really do overlap quite a bit. Often you will hear an agent grousing about managers, how you don't need them. Then that agent will quit or get fired and become a manager, and suddenly, they've had a reawakening. Now, suddenly, you *do* need both.

R. Fox: I have both. I'm not sure exactly what the point of both is, but I'm very non-confrontational, so I guess it'll stay this way until someone leaves me. I know people say, "The agent gets you work and the manager manages your career." Of course, if the agent actually gets you work, your career will already be managed, and vice versa I suppose. It's twice

---

BUZZ WORD

Praisery – A *Variety* term for a public realtions firm: "The studio is retaining an outside prasiery to augment the p.r. chores on the film."

as much money, I know that. But in my mind, however much or little I make, I feel like, "With both of them I got this much, with only one, I'd only have gotten half of that," so I just stay.

S. Susco: I have both, and I'm glad I do. Although many writers don't need managers, I find mine invaluable. While an agent can focus on making sure you've got your next deal coming, a manager can work on your career (usually in sync with the agent) from a more global angle, initiating long-term business relationships, setting short- and long-term goals, and concentrating on *many* irons in the fire instead of just one.

G. McBride: I have multiples of everything. Shortly after selling my first spec, I was lucky enough to land a huge entertainment lawyer. I had no other representation at the time, other than being hip-pocketed at a small agency. My lawyer, who represents pretty much just A-list clients, swears he signed me only to get me to stop faxing him. Hey, whatever works! Anyway, he recommended right away that at this early stage of my career I needed to have as many people trying to sell me and my work as possible. Thus the need for an agent and manager. Of course, this doesn't happen overnight — and you want to get *good* agents and managers, too. You want someone who can be honest with you but who also cares about you. I find managers are more "hands on" and involved in the minute details. Each one works differently, but mine knows *everything* about me and what's going on with my work. Hell, she knows everything about my personal life, too. Between her and my lawyers, I feel like I'm in very good hands. Next add my agents. Though they spend less time with me and are less focused on me as an individual — when they gun for a writing assignment, mine is one in a pile of scripts they're asking producers to read and consider — it's about having as many people keeping an eye on your career as possible. My lawyer's advice has served me well. I think I'll fax him to thank him! Ha!

···

What's the best thing about your agent? The worst?

D. Wallace: I can answer this very simply. The best thing about my agent is that he passionately tries to get me work. The worst thing about my agent is his lack of passion in trying to get me work.

D. Goyer: My current agents were very supportive of my transition into directing. For my first film, *ZigZag*, they weren't afraid of the non-commercial aspects. I made it for a very small budget and effectively worked for free. It took me off the market for an entire year. Frankly, that year was not a profitable one for them. But they stuck with me and now I am directing a much bigger film — now I am a writer-director. Because of their hard work and persistence, I am in a position to do films that I would never have been considered for before.

J. Fasano: The best thing about my representatives is that they are in the trenches, every day, while I'm locked in my house writing, and they know what the business wants. I don't have time for that. The worst thing is that they can be too businesslike — if a script isn't getting a good response, they want to just forget about it, even though I may have worked on it for a year! My feature agent is always looking towards my next spec as the "next big thing" while a shelf of unsold scripts may sit above his desk. If they haven't sold, they're "stale." But there's no freshness date on a good script.

G. McBride: One of the best experiences is when you're being sought after by an agency. For a couple minutes you can even believe your own hype as a "team" of agents goes on and on about your talents and why you should trust them to handle such and such. Of course, it can all change if a spec goes out and doesn't sell. And then it becomes the worst kind of experience — feeling like your "team" doesn't quite believe in you anymore. It's difficult not to take that personally, even though you shouldn't at all. Agents aren't loyal. It's just not in their nature.

R. Fox: He calls me on my birthday. Sometimes he mixes it up with a different client and calls me a full month before my birthday, but it's the thought that counts. He initially tells me everything I write is fabulous and that always feels good. What's the worst part? That's easy. That same script he just loved and e-mailed to tell me just how much, a month later — after he gets four passes — he says, "The piece is problematic." And you start sending him his initial e-mail to remind him of how much he liked it, and he's like, "But the good news is, it's your birthday!"

C. Shyer: Best thing: He's my friend. Worst thing: He's my agent.

....

Have you ever left an agent or manager? Why?

C. Shyer: Oh, please.

G. McBride: Leaving someone who represents you is never an easy decision. But just like in personal relationships, professional relationships are an evolving thing. If you can't change and grow *together* then someone's going to have to ask for a separation.

C. Moss: Yes, we left an agent. He wasn't all that honest about things. Shocker, huh? An agent lying?

J. Fasano: Sometimes it becomes clear that the agent doesn't "get" your work or what you want to do with it. This is the only reason to leave an agent. You can't blame an agent for costing you work if they believe in your talent and ability.

D. Goyer: I left my first agency after both of my agents stopped being agents. Then I left my second agency because I felt they were not responsive to my needs. I was interested in becoming a director and I felt they were being lazy, just booking high-paying writing jobs. It can be difficult to make the transition from writer to director if you are successful as a writer. It means, often, taking a large pay cut for a significant period of time. And agents, being what they are, aren't very keen on that proposition. Of course, ultimately, it's shortsighted. New directors have to come from somewhere and a successful director will be more profitable for an agent. But agents and managers are not always so forward thinking.

D. Wallace: Yes, and for obvious reasons. They weren't doing the job I thought they should be doing, i.e., they weren't selling me on the level and with the dedication I thought was needed. Or, as is more often the case, their sensibilities were wrong for the types of projects I was inclined to write. Agents run hot and cold just like talent runs hot and cold. You've got to be able to judge what's the right temperature for you.

R. Fox: I've left a bunch of agents. I need a lot of coddling. You get that a lot when you first sign with a new agent, just like with a new girlfriend or a new puppy. They keep calling and saying, "This script from five years ago is brilliant, we've got to go back out with this thing, it's gold!" And you feel like, "Well, gee, I thought it was good too, but my old agent said it was 'soft,' or 'it was too similar to something that just flopped.'" Your new agent gives you a look that says, "That was then, now you're with a *real* agent." He sends it out to two places, they both pass — because it's too soft and it's like something that flopped...five years ago — and then he never sends it out again. Then he waits for you to get your own work, and comes in heroically at the final hour and makes you the exact deal you've had four deals in a row.

G. McBride: I have left an agency, and it was because I felt like I fell out of favor with them after a spec script didn't sell. I'm not 100 percent sure this was the reason, of course, but suddenly calls took longer to get returned — if they were returned at all — and attention to my career was down to nothing. At the same time, I tried not to leave bitter. I sent elaborate thank you letters and some good wine to each of the people who had represented me, thanking them for their efforts. But it was time to move on.

S. Susco: Yes, several. I've learned that many agents view their relationship with writers in reverse — that the writer works for them, instead of vice versa. Although this might often feel like the case, a writer must always remember that his or her career is a business, and ultimately *the agent is the employee.* If an agent isn't doing the bare minimum of their job requirement — putting out effort to get you work — then that agent is simply dead weight. If they're not working for you, then they don't really believe in you, and it's time to move on. An agent might talk a big game in order to take you on as a client (as happened to me several times), but the key here is the axiom, "actions, not words." However, writers must also remember that their relationship with an agent is a symbiotic one — the effort must come from both sides. Two many writers assume the agents will do all the work, and all they have to do is sit back and coast. Uh-uh. This is a fatal error. The best way you can help yourself is by helping your agents. And the best way you can help your agents is by making sure you're working as hard — if not harder — than they are.

What do you think about graduate writing programs?

S. Susco: They are what you make of them. If you use the time to master your craft, while banging out as many screenplays as you can, and possibly interning at a production company to learn the "ins and outs" of the biz, then I'm all for them. If you isolate yourself within the program, taking three years to write the "perfect script," and expect agents to be lined up at your door upon graduation, well, then you're selling yourself short.

D. Goyer: Graduate writing programs can be fine — locally, UCLA and USC have good ones, and there are others. But there are other ways to learn how to write. The best way is to simply read other screenplays and start writing. To get feedback. That's critical. Writing really is rewriting. If you only have the stomach to get through a first draft and not get criticism, then you're in the wrong field.

G. McBride: I'm not sure I buy into them. There are writing classes and programs around Los Angeles that I attended when I first moved here, but I found them to be pretty much money-making vehicles and not helpful in the creative process at all. And these were "advanced" classes. They were pretty much worthless. I found that spending time writing is the real education. With each script you write, your writing gets better.

Joe Eszterhas once gave me some amazing advice when I first moved to town: "A writer writes." Simple. Real. True. The best advice anyone's ever given me.

> ## The Director on What Makes a Writer Great
>
> "Writing great scripts is what makes a writer great. There are only two requirements for that — talent and perseverance. Somebody once said, 'This is a business for survivors.' If you're talented, that's great...but you still have to just keep plugging away."
>
> —*Harold Becker*

D. Wallace: I've never been in one, although I know there are some good ones out there. But my take on the educational process is simple and constant. Learn what you can, all you can, wherever you can.

Most importantly write and write some more. If it's a writing program, or just the knowledge of your next-door neighbor, go out there and get what you need.

C. Moss: I'm sure they're fine. Any workshop you can attend to improve your skills is all right in my book...or screenplay. Get it? See, that's comedy right there.

R. Fox: If they make you write more, then I support them. But if you need them to write more, then you probably have no shot of making it. It's a very hard business. If you don't *need* to write, I don't see how you can sustain it. Neil Simon — and I get crazy when people criticize him, I mean, take 20 percent of his work and you still have ten plays and five screenplays that are better than anything anyone else has out there — he was once interviewing himself years ago, and I've always remembered him asking, "Are writers born or made?" He answered, "Born. The ones who are made work well for a few years and then their arms fall off."

. . . .

What does a writer's assistant do? Is this a good way to break in to the business?

C. Shyer: Research. Get coffee. Take the dog to the vet. Is this a good way to break in? Break in to what — writing? No. Writing is the way to break into writing.

D. Goyer: A writer's assistant takes care of the calls and the day-to-day business of running the writer's life — registering scripts, doing research, scheduling meetings, proofreading scripts. It's a very good way to break into writing. Two of my former assistants are now professional writers.

C. Moss: You know what? I don't know. I would think they get laundry or massage your thighs while you write. I've never been one or had one. I would imagine it could be a good way to break in. You can learn a lot from the writer you work for, get an idea of what material works and what doesn't work. The writer might be able to help you get your material seen. Sure...why not?

D. Drake: I have no idea what a writer's assistant does. You might ask Ron Bass. Personally, I think the idea of one is pretty much bullshit. On the other hand, he seems to be doing pretty darn well for himself, so perhaps I should look into getting one.

R. Fox: An assistant's a real luxury if you're on the right project. You pay some kid ten bucks an hour to come over at nine in the morning, bring a nice fresh bagel, he sits on your couch and says, "Okay, let's get to business." So, though you really want to nap and go to the cleaners, you feel like a real jerk spending ten dollars an hour so some guy can watch you talk to your friends on the phone or look up porn sites on the Internet. His most important job is to make sure you stay off the phone. Of course, I say "he," but if your wife will let you have a "she," then all the better. I had a young writer cousin from New York — he was a little narcoleptic and would occasionally put the antenna from the mobile phone in his nose, but other than that, he really helped me get going. I would say, "Hey Rich, what do you think of this?" and if he had a good idea I could use it without crediting him. If he didn't like it, screw him, why would I listen to some guy with a phone in his nose? While you're doing the comedy scenes he's a great addition, but then the problem is when you get to the big emotional moment and you're sitting there at your computer, tears in your eye...and some kid is sleeping on your couch with a phone in his nose, and you just feel like, there has *got* to be better way than this.

As far as *being* someone's assistant, it's a terrific way to get some hands-on experience. Plus, you learn a few of the names and you make some contacts. The writer you work for (if it's me, anyway), probably says things like, "Hey, make sure you let me see your script when you're done and I'll give it to so and so." But mainly, for most of us — regardless of what gifts or sense of humor or imagination we have — it's really about hard work. You can't go back to the "imagination fairy" and ask for more, but when all the other writers go to sleep, you can stay up and keep typing. And the truth is, after all these years and all these scripts, the idea of that still keeps me going the most!

G. McBride: If you're going to be a writer's assistant, I think it would be important to discuss your personal goals with the person you'll be working for. Be direct and let them know that the reason you're willing to run their errands is to learn from them. Commit to being there for them and doing anything for them, but be clear that you have goals and wonder what they think about those goals. If you get a sense that they will throw you a bone every now and then and perhaps help get you an agent in a year or two, then it could be worth it. But again, I suggest being upfront about it from the beginning. It's fair to the writer, and fair to you.

D. Wallace: I've never had a writer's assistant and don't really know that much about them. But any way you can increase your knowledge of the writing process can only be good. Exposure to good writers, no matter how you do that, can only help. So gather all the knowledge you can from whatever sources you can, then run back to your desk and do three things: Write, write, and write some more.

....

What's the biggest mistake you've ever made regarding writing? Best decision?

D. Wallace: That's a tough question, because I don't really believe in mistakes. James Joyce said something to the effect that "All mistakes are just open portals to wisdom." So every perceived mistake is, in my view, just a learning experience that can help you to better your work and yourself. Of course, we don't always learn from our mistakes, so we run the danger of repeating them.

D. Goyer: The biggest mistake I made was trying to write something that I wasn't passionate about. This was an adaptation of the Marvel Comics character, Venom. New Line and Marvel really wanted me to do it and my heart just wasn't in it. But I tried anyway and the results were a disaster. Frankly, the script sucked eggs. It was terrible and everyone knew it. Sometimes you can talk yourself into something, but when you're staring at the page, not feeling it, then it becomes a nightmare.

C. Shyer: The worst decision: to leave my name on a bad movie I had rewritten. The best? To write with Nancy Meyers.

C. Moss: Selling our screenplay to one production company when we should've sold it to another more passionate company. The best decision was to not give up when things looked bleak.

R. Fox: I had an idea for a play, and a studio offered to buy it as a movie. I remember saying to myself, "I've sold a lot of movies, but I've never sold a play." I can still hear myself saying that today, and can't believe it. I could go back, beat my head against the wall, and I still wouldn't believe it. I ended up working five years on the play, did two productions, made 300 trips to New York, and I'm just now going back to the seed of the idea and writing it as a movie. And I'm still in the red on it, too. On the other hand, had I won the Tony, or had the play hit on Broadway...who knows? Maybe I'll still win the Tony. Or maybe I just needed to take that path so I could come back to it now as a movie. It's hard to second-guess yourself. You follow your instincts and sometimes you're right; try to grow from when you're not.

> ## Advice for the Beginning Screenwriter
>
> *"Don't do it!"* Well, actually I would say, *"Absolutely* don't do it!!" I don't even tell people I write screenplays anymore. I find the whole experience a very degrading situation now. The way writers are treated today, I don't understand it. Critics and other people who write about movies are writers, but they still, more often than not, neglect to mention who *wrote* the movie. It's always 'A Film by So-and-So.' To me, that's as ridiculous as saying, above the title, 'Zubin Mehta's Ninth Symphony' and in tiny letters, 'Composed by Beethoven.' It doesn't make any sense. I would say that if you want to maintain any integrity at all, plan to be a director as well as a writer. If you're only doing it for the money, you'll probably make more money smuggling dope."
> —*Arnold Schulman*

D. Drake: Biggest mistake: trying to write with a partner, and in the process wasting my own ideas by giving them away. Best decision: to sit down and do it in the first place, and in the process to trust in the journey and in my own voice.

S. Susco: Worst: taking someone on their word. In this business, make sure all your agreements are *in writing*. Best: ending a partnership that had reached a business zenith, but an emotional nadir.

J. Fasano: The worst mistake I made was walking off *Alien 3* because a writer had been hired after me. If I had done one more draft I would have been in a better position to get credit — which I didn't receive after working on it for over a year — and probably would still talk to producer Walter Hill, who discovered me, but at the time I believed he had abandoned me. Truth was, it was my second Hollywood assignment, one of my dream projects, and I was so hurt someone had been hired after me that I was a complete dick.

Best decision? Moving to Los Angeles. Before coming here, I had directed four features that had been written by other screenwriters. But it was here that I realized I was a writer. If you want to be a lobster fisherman, move to Maine. If you want to write screenplays, come to LA.

G. McBride: Biggest mistake: not being brave enough to move to Los Angeles right after graduating from college. I was scared to take the plunge, and so dove into the world of advertising as my back-up plan. I was still writing specs in my off time, but since advertising kept me away from Los Angeles, I missed the "being here" that is essential to getting that first big break.

Best decision: not being brave enough to move to Los Angeles right after graduating from college. Because I waited to move here, but kept writing specs in my off time, my writing continued to improve. Not to mention I got a few more life experiences under my belt that also lend themselves to story and character.

D. Wallace: The best decision I've made regarding writing was probably the decision to commit to the writing process itself. That's difficult because it's a lifetime commitment, and writing, any kind of writing, is a very uncertain lifestyle. Unfortunately — and unlike novelists or playwrights — screenwriters don't get the kudos they often deserve. Quite often, they're treated like second-class citizens. It's a fluke of the industry that goes way back to the old studio system. It's a travesty and a shame the way writers are often screwed over, when it should be just the opposite way around. Keep this in mind. Everyone in the film business is an interpretive artist — everyone but the writer. He's the only one on any project who starts with the blank page. Everyone else uses his work to base their work on. There is no movie without a writer.

TV WRITERS

How did you break in to TV drama writing?

BARRY GOLD: My first writing credit was for a one-hour drama, though it had a fair amount of humor, called *The White Shadow*. I was just out of college, and thought I wanted to be a TV writer, but knew nothing about it. I had watched the show and really liked it, and had an idea for an episode. So I wrote a spec, and through my aunt, who was then working as a literary agent, I was able to get it to the show's story editor. He liked my writing, but didn't want to do the story. He invited me to pitch other ideas, which I did. By the way, this was over twenty years ago — today, a story editor would never have the power to invite a writer in to pitch. So the story editor liked one of the ideas and told me he'd develop the story, then turn it over to me to write the teleplay. This was really not kosher, but I wasn't in a position to quibble. Eventually he did a two-page outline, which we then re-worked together. I did two drafts of the teleplay, and received that credit, while he took the story credit and money. And, of course, the show that was eventually shot had almost nothing to do with what I had written.

JOHN FASANO: I had written *The Hunchback* as a feature spec. When it didn't sell, my producer suggested trying to sell it to television. Before that I hadn't really given TV any thought. Ironically, I've had some of my best work — *Hunchback, The Hunley, Mean Streak, The Legend of Butch and Sundance, Saving Jessica Lynch* — produced for TV, and on much more varied subject matter than I would have been allowed to in film.

PARIS QUALLES: I was a staff writer on a half-hour comedy and decided to try to change genres. After being told by a number of agents, writers, and producers that I'd be nuts to even attempt it, I plunged in anyway. Knowing that I had to prove to producers and network execs that I could write drama, I wrote a spec script for *China Beach* — a highly respected one-hour show that was on the air at the time. I then found an agent who believed in me to take me on and help me make the transition. They got the spec over to the producers of the show, who read it, liked it, and hired me on staff.

In accomplishing the switch from comedy to drama, I broke through two major myths of television writing: first, that it's near impossible to switch genres, and second, to never expect to get hired on the very show for which you've written a spec.

LARRY BRODY: When I started writing for television, back in the Dark Ages of the '60s, the best way to become a TV writer was to already be acknowledged as a writer in another medium, preferably print because at that time books and the "real writers" who wrote them (as network execs at the time used to say) were highly respected.

I loved television and always wanted to write for it, but I became a "real writer" first, selling poetry, short stories, and a novel while I was still in college. I lived in Chicago and acquired an agent who in turn put me in touch with the late Sylvia Hirsch, then a highly respected agent in the TV Literary Department at William Morris. I wrote a spec screenplay that I hoped would become a movie of the week (that whole genre was just beginning) and sent it to Sylvia, who then asked me to fly out and talk to her. The gist of our meeting was that she believed I had as good a chance of getting a TV writing assignment as anybody she represented. That was good enough for me. I dropped out of grad school and moved to LA.

My real break, however, came through a neighbor in the apartment building I moved into in North Hollywood. Sammy Jackson was an out of work actor who had starred in the Andy Griffith part in the sitcom version of *No Time for Sergeants*. When he heard that I was a writer, he asked me to work up a series idea for him — *any* series idea. I came up with something and wrote a short story featuring the characters and basic situation. Sammy took the story and my spec screenplay to a producer he knew at MGM, and — miracle of miracles! — the producer optioned the short story for a series and liked the writing of the screenplay enough to give me an assignment as co-writer (with an old pro named Arthur Dreifuss, who unfortunately is no longer eating, sleeping, and breathing showbiz — or anything else) on a feature film he was planning. The deals were WGA, which meant that shortly thereafter I was in the Guild — the youngest member of it at the time, or so I was told. I was twenty-three-years-old and had been in Los Angeles for fewer than six months.

The feature was never made, but the fact that I had that kind of professional credit gave Sylvia the ammunition she needed to get me in to see just about everyone who was anyone in the TV drama biz. My first TV show was *Here Come the Brides*, where I was given a crash course in TV writing by the then-story editor Bill Blinn, who has since won Emmy and Peabody Awards, and created a slew of shows. After a few setbacks, my career took off when "relevance" became the watchword in network television. As the only WGA writer young enough to know the current slang, I was automatically an expert on relevance and worked constantly as a freelancer and then a staffer, getting my first producer gig when I was about thirty.

Looking back, it's easy for me to see that my start was a combination of who I was, who I knew, and how I came through when given the chance. If any one of those elements had been missing you wouldn't be asking me questions about TV writing now.

....

How did you break into TV comedy writing?

B. Gold: My first comedy credit was a freelance episode of a show called *Alice*. I had a spec *Taxi* script, which an agent was able to get to the executive producers of *Alice*, Madelyn Davis and Bob Carroll, Jr., famous for their work on *I Love Lucy*. They liked it enough to let me come in to pitch, for which I prepared quite extensively. I recall launching into my first story with something along the lines of, "Okay, it's day, there are four people in the diner, Alice walks in, and..." at which point Bob told me to stop, and then proceeded to give me the best advice I ever got about pitching: "What's the story *in one sentence*?" I took a moment to formulate it, then said, "Mel buys a Porsche for ten dollars." That got their attention, they asked me how that happens — a husband runs off to Brazil with his secretary, tells his wife to sell his Porsche and send him the money, so she lets it go for nothing — and then, along with producers Mark Egan and Marc Solomon, we worked out the story.

P. Qualles: I was doing research for the producers of the show *Amen* and decided to depart from the dry, boring format of the usual research pages. Instead, I read the outline of the story and wrote a scene using dialogue and elements of the research. I turned both in (the scene and the research) to the show's creative consultant and he liked what he saw. A good word was put in for me to the executive producer/showrunner, Ed Weinberger, who hired me on staff as a writer.

· ·

Do I need to live in Los Angeles to write for television?

L. Brody: You can, of course, write anywhere. In fact, as an environment for the actual act of writing, of sitting down and letting your creativity flow from somewhere in the back of your skull to your fingertips as they hit the keyboard, LA isn't all that good. Too many distractions — weather, malls, music, sex — and the worst distraction of all — envy. LA is the city of one-upmanship, where clothes, cars, and neighborhood constantly are compared or flaunted. It's easy to start seeing life as a condition in which your goal is to attain "things" that make your friends and neighbors drool. But as soon as this becomes your prime concern, writing goes tumbling to the bottom of the list. There are, after all, myriad easier and quicker ways to get rich — especially easier.

However, if you want to write for "mainstream media," you've got to be in LA. By mainstream media, I mean the mass market of nationwide broadcasts, cable, and satellite TV. If you're not in LA, you're not going to meet the right "gatekeepers" — the people who can get you a writing job. And you need a writing job because television writing isn't about selling something that's already been written, it's about getting an assignment to write something new for a show that's either on the air or about to get on the air. And yes, even if all you want to do is sell your own series, that's still done on assignment. The way the executives at broadcast networks and cable and satellite channels look at it, they're developing your idea with you. Of course, the way most writers look at it, the execs are destroying the idea for you, which is why I've become such a strong advocate of alternate media...if only I could figure out what those alternates were.

Actually, if you don't mind the brain-rotting distractions, living in LA can be terrific. It is, after all, the place where the showbiz lifestyle reaches its apex, so even if you don't make it, there's always going to be something to laugh at.

P. Qualles: It depends on the kind of writing. A general rule of thumb is to live in or near the city that produces the type of programming you want to write, and where the creative executives at the networks and studios are based. Dramatic and comedic productions are generally based in the Los Angeles area. News and soap writers generally live in the New York area. Long-form writers can generally live in either. Feature film writers can live anywhere, but being in or near one of the two centers is helpful when just starting out. The key is to be flexible enough to take meetings at a moment's notice. Unless you live in the city of the meeting, having the money and flexibility to travel for a pitch can be a problem.

A big exception to the above is staff writing for distant location-based productions. A series might be shot in Vancouver, Toronto, or New York City, but the writing staff is based in Los Angeles.

B. Gold: Because there's so much group work on series television, I do think you need to live in Los Angeles. Maybe someday the technology will allow staff writers to live elsewhere, but I think that's a ways off.

....

How many sample spec scripts do I need to break into the industry? What are good shows to spec? How current does a spec need to be?

P. Qualles: One *good* spec script is all you need to get a job. However, to convince an agent or producer that, a) you're looking for a career, b) you're more than a one-hit wonder, and c) you have a work ethic, it's always desirable to have a body of work. Any show that is respected and currently on the air is fine to spec. If a show's been off the air for four years, chances are the reader will wonder why you're submitting such old material. Also, the reader may not know or remember enough about the series to evaluate your writing. A spec should be as current as the series it's based on. And a quality, popular show is preferable to a quality, obscure one because the reader is more likely to know the show's format, characters, and tone, and consequently be better able to judge your treatment of it.

B. Gold: I always felt like you needed at least two spec scripts. If someone likes your work, they might want to read something else to make sure it wasn't a fluke, or to see if you can handle different types of shows. As far as what to spec, that changes year to year. My sense is you want to do a show that's fresh — probably one that's in its first or second year. And it should be a show that's not just popular, but is also considered good quality. Most importantly, it should be a show you're comfortable with, that suits your sensibility. It's very hard to fake it on a show that's not your style. As for how current your specs should be, my feeling is a writer trying to break in needs to be writing new scripts every season. If you're on the outside trying to get in, it doesn't look good to be circulating a five-year-old spec of a long dead series. It shows a lack of effort, and not much ambition. Plus, you should get better with every script you write, so it's to your advantage to keep producing new material.

L. Brody: To break into the television today, a writer needs three spec teleplays and a spec screenplay. In television, the drama/action business and the sitcom business are, for all practical purposes, two different industries. So the first thing you should do as a beginner is decide which of those two genres you want to pursue. Then write spec episodes for three different shows in your genre, as well as a screenplay in that genre. The shows should be as current as can be and you should follow the continuity for that season.

I speak from experience when I say that showrunners are looking for writers who can, in effect, "ghostwrite" for them. It's not really ghostwriting because if you're hired you'll get screen credit — the idea is to write not in your own style *but in the closest possible approximation of the showrunner's* — because the showrunner's style is what's being produced. It's why he or she was hired. It's what they are expected to give the network. That means that to a showrunner the definition of a good writer is simple: "By God, they better write just like me!"

This isn't quite the straitjacket it seems. Within the practical constraints of TV, a new writer does have a way of showing versatility. If you're a drama/action writer, for example, write one spec for a critically acclaimed "serious" drama, making it as close to the real deal as you can. Then write a spec for a balls-out action show, also making it as close to the source as possible. Your third spec should be for a family drama, written also just as though you were the current showrunner. But your spec screenplay should be the real you, writing as yourself and presenting an issue and storyline about which you feel passionate — because how the hell else are you going to be able to write a whole 110 pages? Some showrunners will read only spec screenplays because then they know that what they're seeing is the absolute best you can do.

Likewise, if you see yourself as a sitcom writer, write one spec for a critically acclaimed "sophisticated comedy," another for the silliest show you can stand, and a third for, well, whatever's in-between. Again, make them as much like the series they're based on as possible. Then write a spec screenplay that's a comedy, too. Write it your way. Express yourself, and your native comic rhythm. A little free advice here, to paraphrase Garry Marshall, "We already have writers who write as good as anything already on TV. What we need are writers who write better." So make sure everything you write really is better. Be brilliant. Write with such skill that no one can turn you down.

· ·

Does having a feature spec script help me get TV writing work?

B. Gold: I have heard that a feature spec can help you get TV work, but I believe it's most likely to help in the one-hour drama area.

P. Qualles: Depends on the reader and genre. If you're interested in long-form, it will help prove you can write the form as the formats are close enough. Episodic series readers (especially at the producer level and above) are usually an eclectic bunch who will sometimes read "off-genre" stuff — e.g., stage plays, documentaries, or even poems — to assess talent. If sitcoms are your bag, the spec feature had better be a laugh-out-loud comedy, and, harder still, it better be sustainable over the two-hour script. Better to try to sell your feature spec as a feature and write some series specs specific to the series genre.

••

What is a showrunner?

P. Qualles: Basically, a showrunner is the person who runs the show. He or she is usually the "real" executive producer as well as being the head writer, although not necessarily always the latter. Showrunners are the real power in series television. They interface with network and studio execs, hire and fire staff, crew, and cast, and are largely responsible for the look, feel, and operation of the show. It's a highly skilled job, meshing politics, organizational skills, and time management. Unlike the various producer titles — including "Executive Producer" — bestowed on those often undeserving of the credit, the showrunner position is earned only after toiling in lesser positions on previous shows. It can take years to acquire the experience and skills, and there is no template or training program to help, although the Writer's Guild is working on one. You can't fake the position and it's sometimes questionable that the considerable money showrunners earn is worth the stress, strain, and aggravation.

B. Gold: A showrunner is the executive producer who makes the final decisions in regards to a television series. He or she decides which stories will be done, how they'll be done, who will write them, and probably either does the final rewrite on a script or tells someone else what to do. The showrunner also makes the decisions about script changes during production, and makes casting and editing decisions as well. In a way, the showrunner is the King or Queen — of course, even royalty has to answer to God, or in this case, the network and the studio executives. Most showrunners rise to that position due to their writing talents, but the job also requires management skills. Frankly, not many people have both. I was very fortunate to work for Rick Hawkins at *Major Dad*, who was very talented in both areas, which led to a joyful work experience. When the showrunner isn't a good manager, expect long hours and much frustration. But be glad you've got a job, most people don't.

L. Brody: A showrunner is a writer who has been put in charge of all creative aspects of a television series. Once upon a time the showrunner was simply called the "producer" and he or she wasn't necessarily a writer but rather a seasoned media professional who knew how to develop a good script and give it the production values it deserved at a reasonable price. As more TV writers realized that as writers they had very little clout — and pretty poor sex lives because other people working in Hollywood had already figured out that writers couldn't help their careers — we started demanding to be made producers. The stated reason was to protect our writing from bad production. The real reason was, well, the sex thing. Okay, let's be more circumspect and call it "power." Another reason writers started to be made producers was that studios and networks got away with paying a smaller percentage of contributions for WGA health and pension benefits for producers than for staff writers or story editors — a situation that exists to this day.

As more writers became producers and more shows had more and more producers, the old-time producers vanished, swept away by the tide. And the writers with the most clout became showrunners, first in fact and then as an informal title that has now settled into a more formal one. The showrunner supervises all the script development for a series and usually is the final rewriter of each episode. The showrunner also oversees the casting, sets, hiring of directors, and just about everything else you can think of that effects what the viewers see on their television sets. Good showrunners not only are the most creative people you'll find working in television today, they're also master politicians and salesmen, spending an enormous amount of time placating stars and networks, and positioning themselves for their next show or job. Showrunners of successful — and sometimes unsuccessful — series often are paid a fortune, but they put in hours that people in other occupations would find unimaginable. These people *work* for their money.

••

Will any production company look at my material without representation?

L. Brody: To answer that I have to let you in on a basic truth of showbiz, one that most people in the industry deny publicly but admit privately. This is it: No one in feature films or television is really looking for new writers. Nor are they looking for new material.

New writers are a huge gamble. "What if she doesn't deliver?" "What if he delivers late?" "What if they don't write it the way I want it and *need* it to be written?" The answer to all those questions, for the hiring executive or producer is, "I'm screwed, that's what." The potential performance of known writers, "old pros," can be gauged based on past experience. Writer A is a good "starter" but will need to be rewritten. Writer B isn't funny enough, but the story is there. Writer C will sacrifice all story logic for the sake of a good joke. Writer D's work always comes in on time but lacks passion. Writer E's work is passionate as all hell but will be three weeks late. And so on. When you hire a known writer with known strengths and weaknesses, then you know how to plan ahead, what to prepare for. But when you hire a new writer everything's unpredictable, and it can be mighty tough justifying the hire to a boss who says, "Why didn't you have my sister-in-law write it, for God's sake? She'd at least give us a great, teary, finale — even if nobody can understand how she got there!"

New material can be an even bigger risk. No matter how brilliant a new genre or storyline may be, there's no way to judge whether the public will accept it — as in no way to determine in advance what the potential ratings or earnings will be. Ergo, no reason to even start down that path.

Why then do all the production companies, networks, and studios have so many people whose job descriptions say they're supposed to be reading new material by new writers? Some insiders say it's a matter of "just in case," that the thinking goes, "We're reading new stuff just in case something so brilliant that it can't miss comes along, written by somebody so brilliant that he can't miss either." Others think it's just tradition. "Hey, the jobs exist. They've always existed. Know the trouble we could get into for changing that?" Especially when so many big shots have started as readers and development folks. They know that this department is the perfect training ground. After all, look what it did for them. Besides, it relieves a lot of pressure from friends, neighbors, relatives, and other VIPs who either want to be writers or know someone who does. "Sure," the exec can say, "send in a sample of her work. I'll have my assistant take a look-see."

Armed with this new insight, let's go back to the questions: "Will any production company look at my material if I don't have representation?" Now the answer should be obvious: not goddamn likely. Production companies are always looking for excuses to dodge the bullet and say no. If you don't have an agent, you've given them Excuse Number One.

That's not to say that it's impossible to be read if you don't have an agent or manager. On the contrary, if you're a friend, neighbor, relative, or some kind of VIP, your work will still be read because that's what the readers are there for. And if you're very persistent and very charming and get someone at the company to like you enough to vouch for you, the likelihood is that you'll get read then, too — after signing what's called a "release," which is a piece of paper in which you swear you won't sue them if they steal your work. Nice, huh? But then again, if you're charming and get someone to like you enough to vouch for you, guess what? You're still not an exception. You've simply moved into the category of "friend."

P. Qualles: Most won't. Liability is the biggest problem. And execs also don't have a lot of time to waste. It takes just as much time to read a bad script as a good one, and there are many more of the former. Execs at production companies will generally not read any material that doesn't come from an agent or agency known to them. There are exceptions. For instance, if the exec is doing a favor and reading his dentist's wife's brother's script, or another exec recommends the material. Even so, liability is still an issue and a signed "Release of Liability" document is often required before the material can be received. The vast majority of scripts are sent to execs via agents, so the strategy of the newbie writer should be to secure representation *in addition* to attempting to get anyone and everyone who can help to read their script.

B. Gold: I guess shows occasionally flat-out buy scripts from outside writers, but I've only seen it happen once. And that woman was immediately added to the show's staff. I've always heard that you shouldn't even show your spec of a particular show to that show's producers, as they're more likely to find all the flaws and they probably don't want to believe an outsider could write their show as well as they do, either.

BUZZ WORD

Tyro – In general, someone new to a field or activity; in *Variety*, a first-time director, writer, etc.: "Written by tyro scribes Dan Wilson and David Gilbreth, pic is the story of two genius brothers."

Do shows that have writing staffs also buy scripts from non-staff writers?

P. Qualles: Yes. Due to the perennially high unemployment of writers at any given time, the Writer's Guild requires most shows that produce scripted material to hire at least a small number of "freelance" writers, writers who are current guild members but not staffing a show. Non-staff writers, and even non-guild members, can also sometimes sell a component of the script, such as the story, for payment. Although in that case, the actual teleplay is often still written by the staff.

L. Brody: These days all mainstream media television shows have writing staffs of three to ten people. I don't know of any that "buy" episodic scripts from outside or non-staff writers. But then, I also don't know of any television series that has ever made a regular practice of "buying" a script from anyone. It's always been an assignment business. Get yourself a meeting with whoever can authorize an episode. Tell him or her a few ideas you've got for potential episodes of their series — the infamous "pitch meeting." Get assigned to write one or more of those ideas as scripts. That's how it has always worked.

Once upon a time, though, freelance writers wrote 90 percent of the episodes. Now they write less than 10 percent. The WGA says every series has to meet with a certain number of freelancers each season. It doesn't say any of those freelancers have to be *hired*. These meetings and the occasional freelance assignment that comes out of them, however, are one of the ways out-

> ### Why shouldn't I show my spec of a particular TV show to that show's producers?
>
> This is now the practice, and it's done to protect the writer. No one knows the show like the people writing it. So the feeling is, if you spec a *Sopranos* or *Six Feet Under*, the staff there will look at it and focus only on what's not working instead of what is. They may have whole plot lines worked out for a character's arc that you won't be aware of, and then you have the character do something they feel she'd never do. It's like setting yourself up for failure. But if you spec a show that's similar in tone to the one you want to write for, the producers won't know that show as well and will be able to focus on the good writing.
>
> —*Linda Cowgill*

side writers eventually get in — that is, get on staff. Tell a sensational story, something no staff member has thought of. Get the assignment. Write the hell out of it, and voila! — you're a freelancer no more, now you're a staff writer. What I'm saying is that even though the odds are against you, take whatever meeting you can and pitch, pitch, pitch whenever you can to whomever you can. Because when things come together, they come together very, very well.

....

How do I find out if a show is open to outside submissions?

B. Gold: I don't think shows are really *open* to submissions. Most will use a few freelance writers per the WGA requirements during a season, and the key is getting a chance to pitch your story ideas. It's up to your agent to get your material to someone at the show, and hope they'll be impressed enough to let you come in for a meeting.

L. Brody: It's not hard. Call the office of the production company (you'll see its name in the credits at the end of each episode), ask for the executive producer (or showrunner), and when the assistant answers — ask. Be charming and polite and who knows? Maybe the assistant will help you in other ways. Maybe the two of you will fall in love. Maybe not.

P. Qualles: Call the show directly and ask. Can't hurt. You can also check with various publications, such as *Written By*, *Hollywood Reporter*, and *Daily Variety*. They'll often list all the current shows in production and their execs. Agents are also a good source for this information.

....

How are story ideas created for a series?

B. Gold: In my experience, stories are suggested by anyone on the staff, from the showrunner on down. They're often discussed in a group —

BUZZ WORD
Pitch meeting – A meeting with a producer or studio executive in which you sell them your story idea, generally for an unwritten project.

there's an effort to "get the shape" of the story, and if the showrunner thinks it's worth doing, it gets blocked out scene-by-scene.

P. Qualles: Story ideas are usually generated either by a member of the writing staff alone, jointly by the staff, or by a freelance writer in for a pitch. On series with recurring stories or arcs, episodes are often preordained.

. . . .

Once you get an assignment as staff writer, run through the process of what happens next. Do all the writers contribute to your script? Who has the ultimate decision on whether the script will be shot or not?

P. Qualles: Depends on the show. Usually, the story is worked out by committee and the writer is then sent off to write a first draft. If the production workload is high or the staff writer has a good track record of developing stories solo, he or she may be given the greenlight to go and develop the story alone. Unless there's a production crisis and a shootable script is needed immediately, usually only one or two other staffers may be assigned to help out by rewriting or taking portions of the script to work on. The head writer or showrunner will often take the final pass before it's submitted to the network for approval. The ultimate decision of production is the networks.

B. Gold: Often the writer who suggested the original idea will be assigned to write it, but it could be assigned on a rotation basis, or through some other method. I don't feel that writers on staff "own" their suggestions — coming up with ideas is part of why they're being paid a weekly salary. The assigned writer will go away to do a story outline, which will then be distributed to the group. Everyone contributes story notes, the showrunner deciding which are worth taking and which are not. Once the story is set, the writer is now responsible for producing a first draft, which could be due tomorrow on a poorly run show, or in several weeks. Then the script is read by everyone, and once more notes are given. The writer may do another draft, or a different writer may take a crack at it, or scenes may be divided up; there are many ways to go. Eventually, however, the showrunner will make the final changes to the script, and then have to deal with the network, studio, stars, managers, etc. — all of whom have other ideas.

....

I have a TV pilot script. How do I go about selling it?

B. Gold: My sense is that it's very hard to sell a spec pilot script, maybe because I've never done so. I guess it can happen, but you hear of it very rarely, and then by people who are already well established. I believe *Malcolm in the Middle* was a spec pilot, written by the already very successful Linwood Boomer.

P. Qualles: If you're not established in the industry, know that you have a tough road ahead. Consider the difficulties that established creators such as John Wells, Steven Bochco, or Diane English have in selling pilots to networks and you see the problem a newbie writer is going to have just trying to get in the door.

If the series idea is good enough, my recommendation is to get the idea to an established writer-producer or production company and let them use their clout to run it up the network flagpole. In this scenario, it's also a good idea to lower your own expectations as to your involvement in the event that the idea does sell. It's not likely you will write the pilot, get a "Created by" or "Developed by", or even a low-level producer credit if the show — against all odds — makes it on the air. More likely you'll just get a staff writing position.

L. Brody: This is the Big Question for everyone interested in television. Whether we're beginners, staff writers, showrunners, whatever, we all want to sell our own series. Everyone who watches television has an idea for a series that they're certain will be a hit. When you consider that we're talking about over 200 million people in the US alone, you know you're really up against it.

The fact that you've actually written the thing puts you ahead of about 199,999,900 people in the US. But for mainstream American television, this isn't as big a deal as it seems. For current broadcast networks, cable channels, and satellite channels, most new series come out of what's known as the "development process." Someone who can write or otherwise provide content, pitches the idea for a show to someone who can buy or otherwise put a show on the air. If the buyers like the idea, then they work out the whole series idea together — with other executive-type participants as well. A danger in writing a pilot script is that you might take an idea in a direction that a buyer — who otherwise would be interested — detests, which means that the buyer will pass. Besides, you want to get paid for writing the script, don't you? And you do get paid if you "develop" it with a network, studio, production company, etc.

In mainstream media, showrunners of current or recent hits are the series creators of choice. They're the stars the execs want to fuck. Most showrunners are rewarded for their success by getting deals for new series well in advance of creating them. The hottest even get commitments. That's right, they get a guaranteed number of episodes and a guaranteed time slot at a guaranteed budget and rate of pay for an idea *still to be determined*. Production companies or studios producing current or recent hits often get the same kind of deal. This means that most of the new shows that appear each fall come from that group.

Most of the other new series come from established pros working with hot studios or companies. Often the pros are producers a step or two below the showrunner who have gained the networks' or cable channels' confidence and are now being brought up a notch. The few remaining slots for new series get filled by writers — again, mostly known commodities — who have come in and pitched and managed to strike gold.

Sometimes a total outsider scores. Chris Carter of *The X-Files* had no television experience when he sold that series to Fox. Other times a fully shot pilot makes it big. Many of the current non-fiction "lifestyle" shows originated that way. Contests, both online and off, are also helping new writers make strides in selling their own series ideas. Some guarantee production as a prize. Others have become so well-known that high placement is the same as having solid, respected professional credits, thus getting the winner in the door.

Speaking of fully shot pilots, I see this as the wave of the future, a chance to get past the showrunner star system currently in place. As someone who has loved television since the first time I saw Howdy Doody yelling, "Watch out, Buffalo Bob, Clarabelle's going to squirt you!" I want what's best for both the writer and the medium. Fulfilling commitments and bringing writers up through the ranks are both excellent ways to make sure that what's on TV is the same old-same old. These techniques keep the tried and true firmly in place. But is that good for television? Is that good for those who want to write television? Shouldn't we be reaching out and trying to create shows that are fresh and creative and exciting in ways no one could even imagine before they arrived?

To me, the answer to that is, "Yes!" Artistically very little has changed since the late 1940s, when the modern era of TV broadcasting began. The result is that the percentage of the overall population that watches TV has dropped considerably since the 1960s, when television sets became ubiquitous, and the percentage of those satisfied with what they're watching has dropped even more. Change has to come from new people — people whose creative energies haven't been co-opted by the system.

My biggest regret, careerwise, was a decision I made when I first started. There were all kinds of new shows jostling for a place in my mind but when they received a bad reception I told myself, "All right, I get it. I'll do what they want now, in order to get started. And then when I'm 'someone' I'll use my new power and position to do what I want."

Well, hey, fans, guess what? When I reached that position I discovered that the only reason I held it was because I was giving the powers that be what they wanted. I was a certain kind of cop/detective/lawyer/doctor writer, and my new ideas (really my original ones) still fell on deaf ears. Just about any showrunner will admit that if he or she pushes too hard for the kinds of things those who elevated him don't like, the execs will knock him right off his perch. After all, with so many people wanting to run shows, who needs someone who's a pain in the ass?

But current technological advances bring with them more hope. Why write the usual crap for the usual suspects? In fact, why just write? For under $5000 anyone can have the video hardware and software necessary to shoot and edit their own film or pilot — or a zillion episodes based on that pilot. Everyone's got friends who think they should be actors, or talk show hosts. Use them to shoot your own shows.

Let me say that again. Make your own shows, the ones you've been dreaming about forever. Take the finished products to the networks, the cable channels, the satellite systems, the syndicators. Put them online.

BUZZ WORD

Overall deal – Also known as a housekeeping deal, an overall deal is one in which a producer or production company is given office space on the lot and a (sometimes lavish) budget with which to run it while not being attached to any specific project.

Advertise in niche magazines and sell your stuff by mail. Be really bold and sell it at Wal-Mart. Create what you want to create the way you want to create it. Distribute your work the way you need to distribute it. In this way video production becomes what literature once was — art for the masses. Hell, Thoreau and Emerson gave away their essays. Think of how much you could give to posterity by giving away your short films.

And remember this. One of the best things about life is that, contrary to what most people believe, it is not an "either/or" proposition. There are never just two choices. There are an infinite number of possibilities at every fork in life's road. You can take the creative way, the entrepreneurial art and self-expression route, while simultaneously continuing to try to score with mainstream media. As a wise man once said, "Life is so filled with possibilities it makes everything amazing. Both the good and the bad fill me with wonder. Just by having the experience, you win even when you lose." Okay, so Jeff Bridges, an actor, said it. He's still a wise man — because if you take the media challenges head-on everyone else can win with you.

The Ins and Outs of TV Series Writer Deals

The television business has undergone a dramatic change in recent years. In the past, studios would lavishly spend millions of dollars on long-term development deals with TV writers, referred to as "overall deals," in the hope that during the two to four year terms of such arrangements, while the studio is paying the writer's overhead plus a salary, the writer will create a hit show for the studio. Those days are now gone — unless of course, you're Dick Wolf or David Kelley!

Nowadays, a writer is typically engaged to perform the initial step of writing a pilot script, and the studio is granted a number of options to engage the writer to render additional services on the pilot episode and/or series, both writing and producing. The benefit of this arrangement to the studio is clear: if the studio is not happy with the script, it can cut its losses relatively early, having committed only to payment of the initial script fee. Such deals, referred to as "one-offs," used to represent only a fraction of the deals that studios would enter into when developing television pilots and series, but are now the dominant form

➡

of television series writing deals. To give you an idea of what we're talking about and a heads-up for important things to consider when you're negotiating a deal, below is the basic outline of a television "one-off" pilot or series writing agreement:

Pilot Writing Fee: The first item you would negotiate in connection with these types of agreements is invariably the pilot scriptwriting fee. Under the WGA Agreement — which governs most television projects, as all of the major networks are Guild signatories — union minimum, or "scale," for such services is approximately $30,000 for a half hour script and $43,000 for a sixty-minute script. For scale, the studio is entitled to a story, first draft, and final draft of the script — also called a teleplay. In most instances, the studio will bargain for a story, first draft, two sets of revisions, and a polish. Usually, the writer/creator will receive more than scale and pilot writing fees can range from $50,000 for a relatively inexperienced writer, to $250,000 or higher for an A-level television writer — i.e., one who has already created at least one successful series, such as David Milch. As we mentioned above, this is the only money that the writer is guaranteed to receive under the "one-off" deal.

Pilot Producing Services: The next issue of negotiation you would need to concern yourself with is the nature of the writer's services, if any, in the event that your script is well-received and the pilot episode is ordered to production. In many cases, the studio will guarantee the writer employment as an "executive producer" of the pilot episode at a negotiated fee. Other times — for example, if the pilot writer is not an established television writer or showrunner — the studio might agree to attach the writer to the project at a lower level, such as a consulting or supervising producer. The writer's role in connection with the pilot is ultimately a result of negotiation, taking into account the writer's clout and prior experience. The WGA does not govern producing fees, as such services are not deemed to constitute writing. The fees for such producing services can range anywhere from $15,000 to $100,000.

Series Services and Compensation: If the pilot is "picked up" by the network, that is to say that series episodes are ordered to production, then the studio can choose to exercise its option — negotiated up front, as part of the "one-off" deal — to engage the writer as some type of producer on the series. A writer's series episodic producer fee will generally be lower than the pilot producing fee, as there is less work to do once the first episode — the pilot — is completed.

➡

Another point that is negotiated as part of the pilot/series deal is the length of time that that the pilot writer (or "series creator") will be "locked" or attached to the series, thereby continuing to receive screen credit and a fee. A studio will usually agree to lock the writer/creator to the series for at least one year and in many cases two. Again, this depends largely on the writer's status in the television industry. Top writer-producers, such as Steven Bochco, might be guaranteed an executive producer fee and credit for the "life" of the series. A writer/creator might also be guaranteed the opportunity to write, and be paid for, a specified number of episodic scripts during each year of the series.

In addition to series producing fees, you may negotiate for a "series sales bonus," which is a sum of money payable as a bonus if and when the network orders series episodes based on the pilot. While the dollar amount of a series sales bonus will vary and is subject to negotiation, it is fairly standard today for a series sales bonus of $25,000 to be granted in the event the writer receives sole "written by" credit on the pilot and sole "created by" credit on the series. This bonus may be reduced if the writer receives shared credit and/or if less than a set number of episodes, usually twelve, are actually produced.

Finally, the WGA Agreement requires that the writer or writers accorded "created by" credit on a series receive a royalty, or payment, for each episode of the series that is produced beyond the pilot. The current WGA required royalty for network prime-time programming is approximately $1,000 per episode. Subject to this minimum, the actual amount of the royalty payable to the series creator is negotiable and may be as high as $6,000 per episode for top guns.

Profit Participation: A writer's profit participation in a television project is typically more significant than with respect to a feature film, and is more likely to generate payment to the writer for two reasons. First, as a television writer, you can normally negotiate for a percentage of the profits in excess of 5 percent, which is the standard participation for motion picture writers with limited exceptions. In addition, television writers are generally more successful than their feature film counterparts in extracting favorable terms from the studios relating to the calculation of such profits. Second, an enormously successful series may generate so much cash relative to its costs, that regardless of the precise definition of the project's "net proceeds," it is likely to generate some payment in many cases.

➡

We think it is therefore imperative for a writer's representative to take great care in negotiating the definition of "project proceeds" in the writer's contract. A top-level showrunner/creator will often be able to negotiate for 15 percent or more of the "adjusted gross receipts" — gross revenues less certain defined deductions and a reduced distribution fee — or for up to 50 percent of the "net proceeds," reducible by net participations granted to third parties. If a project survives the uphill battle toward syndication, these profits may indeed materialize.

Credit: Assuming that the production falls within the WGA's jurisdiction, the Writer's Guild Agreement will determine the form of most writing credits. Typically, the writer or writers receiving "written by" or "story by" credit on the pilot will be accorded a "created by" credit on the series. The WGA does not, however, govern producing credits. The terms and conditions relating to the writer's "executive producer" or "supervising producer" or even "consultant" credit need to be specifically addressed by contract. In recent years, a number of established writers have requested "logo" credits (which will typically appear in the end titles) in addition to their producer credits. For example, a "Chase Films" logo appears at the end of every episode of *The Sopranos* at the request of that series' creator, David Chase.

Perks: As is the case with most talent agreements, writers can usually negotiate for some basic "perks" (which may or may not be granted, depending upon their status), such as first-class travel and accommodations, per-diem, and ground transportation to and from airports, hotels, and sets if the studio or network requires the writer to travel on location. In addition, some writers request that the studio provide an exclusive office and assistant during all periods in which they are expected to render exclusive services. Finally, a reserved parking space is considered a bit of a status symbol in Hollywood and is requested by most series creators.

This is merely a brief overview of television pilot and series writer agreements. Terms and conditions can vary from deal to deal. Before signing any contract, we strongly recommended that writers consult with an experienced entertainment attorney who can review the agreement in detail.

—Dina Appleton and Daniel Yankelevits

ASK THE PROS
DEVELOPMENT

PRODUCERS, DEVELOPMENT & STUDIO EXECS

How do you decide if a spec screenplay or other property is one you want to develop?

STANLEY M. BROOKS (Television Producer): In real estate they say the deciding factor should be location, location, location. In the TV movie business it's concept, concept, concept. We're looking for that "big idea." The concept is the poster is the movie. If it doesn't sell itself in one or two sentences, we probably won't be able to sell it. Movies for television don't have the advantage of "word of mouth," they have to hit in one night, so on-air promos are the most powerful marketing tool we have. If you can't sell the film in thirty seconds, it doesn't work for us. That is our chief criterion when deciding what material to pursue.

HAROLD BECKER (Producer-Director): I have to like the story, that's the first thing, it has to be a story that appeals to my sensibility. Then the writing has to fulfill the story being told. It has to be equal to the story. It's no good having a great story and not having writing that is commensurate to it. So I'd say my interest is determined by whether the story engages me and if the writing is of a nature that makes me want to turn the page.

KEN KOKIN (Producer): I look for material with layers, something that will make the audience see the subject in a new light or as something with artistic merit.

MYRL A. SCHREIBMAN (Producer): The focus for a screenplay must be on the story and the characters. If the screenplay "jumps" off the page — which is to say that the characters are interesting and vivid — I know that the project will be attractive to others who will help get the picture made. This involves dialogue that is true to the characters and not just there to advance the plot. It must enhance the relationships of the story.

DAN STRONCAK (Creative Executive): It's decided by our development team. We discuss the types of material we need to fulfill our studio deal and then we all look for material to match those needs. When someone on the team finds something they like, then the rest of the development team reads it and we discuss it in our staff meeting. If we all see potential, then we will option or buy the material.

DAVID T. FRIENDLY (Producer): First there has to be a consensus at the company that we all believe in the idea. That's first and foremost, the most important thing, because you can always fix the script, but you can't always fix an idea. The fundamental questions we ask are: What is the core idea? Does it have a strong enough hook and a strong enough concept? Who will the movie appeal to? Why do we want to make it? These are the most important things we use in evaluating a spec. The writing is important, but not as important as the idea.

> *Could you list some scripts you wish all spec screenwriters would read as excellent examples of what you look for in a spec screenplay?*
>
> The first script that comes to mind is *American Beauty* because I read it the first night it went out to the town. I remember thinking, "Now *this* is how every spec script should read." The characters were three-dimensional, unique, and compelling. There were amazing conflicts, character arcs, and surprises. It was a great script that didn't change much from its first draft to the actual film. I also think *Meet The Parents* and *Erin Brockovich* are good specs to read. I think you're smart to look at good writing and to study the writer's techniques, characters, and structure.
> —*Chrissy Blumenthal*

PETER MILLER (Producer-Manager): We look for larger-than-life stories that are character-driven and of outstanding quality.

SETH SCHUR (Development Executive): If there's a role for Ernest Borgnine, we're in! Honestly though, our criteria changes from time to time depending on the profile of our development slate. The genre, size, and scope of the project are certainly factors. Being that we have produced some darker and smaller-sized movies recently, we are looking for more commercially viable material at the moment — something that will appeal to a wide range of moviegoers. We're drawn to projects that utilize a great idea or concept that is fresh and original but which also draw on familiar themes that people can relate to. *The Sixth Sense* is an example of a movie with a great concept that succeeded to the level that it did because it was more than just a ghost story — it explored the nuances of relationships at a very human level.

. . . .

How do you prioritize the material submitted to you through legitimate sources?

STEPHANIE PALMER (Studio Executive): Of the ten to twenty submissions I get per week, I prioritize based on who has submitted the script, the concept, and the author. The easiest way to get me to read a script is if I am already a fan of the author's work. Second most important is if I have worked with the submitting producer or agent previously and had a positive experience. If I don't know the submitting producer well, but the concept of the project is intriguing, then I will definitely read the material. If the script is 0 for 3 in these categories, then it's rare that I will have a chance to read it due to the high volume of material submitted that *does* have attractive elements.

M. Schreibman: This is clearly based upon my relationships. I always prioritize based upon the relationship I have with the person who provides me with the material. This is true in most cases with other people as well. For example, the script for the film *Duplex* was given to Danny DeVito by Drew Barrymore and Ben Stiller as a project that would interest DeVito with both of them in the cast. DeVito knew Stiller from working with him and he knew Barrymore from the *ET* days. The relationship was symbiotic and fell into place.

D. Stroncak: We spend a lot of time establishing relationships with agents and managers, which allows us to get material that fits what we're looking for. We don't generally get into bidding wars because we're not chasing specs that go out wide. We spend more time developing material and putting a package together before taking it into the studio.

S. Brooks: We prioritize based on our current needs. By and large, we seek out specific material. We'll call our ten to twenty favorite agents and agencies, and request a specific genre. We also prioritize by relationship. If a script or story comes in from a writer we have already worked with, that will always come first.

S. Schur: We prioritize based on the time sensitivity and the level of talent involved with the project. If it's a spec, we look at it right away due to the fact that we could lose out on a good project to another producer if we don't act quickly. If it's not a spec and there aren't any specific time restraints, we'll prioritize based on the level of writer or attachments. We're going to look at something from an established writer or something with a filmmaker attached before we look at something from an unknown writer from the Podunk Literary Agency.

....

How much weight does coverage have? How much does coverage affect your decisions?

D. Stroncak: Readers are the gatekeepers. Busy execs don't have time to read all the scripts that come across their desks so readers and coverage are very important. I trust my readers and generally go with their recommendations.

M. Schreibman: I personally believe coverage is a waste of time. Coverage *never* affects my decision. The people who provide coverage often only include the plot in their coverage and rarely discuss the quality of the dialogue. They are often also frustrated writers or producers and unconsciously put themselves into the role of writer in terms of evaluating the material. I have seen readers dump on excellent scripts because they did not write them. This is unfair to the work being evaluated.

P. Miller: Since we're primarily in the intellectual property business, coverage is very important. But then we always ask the question, "Who did the coverage?"

CHRISSY BLUMENTHAL (Producer): It depends on the reader. If the reader is highly experienced, has worked with our company before and is one whose opinion I trust, then the coverage could weigh heavily on my decision to even read the script. If coverage comes back as a "pass," I will read ten pages of the script to see if I agree with the reader. If, after ten pages, I still like it, I will continue the script. Also, if the script is a "pass" but I like the premise, I will read the script to see if it's something that can be re-written. If a script comes back with a "consider," I will most likely read the entire script. However, if I start reading the script and I don't agree with the reader, I can glance at coverage again to see how the story unfolds and from there I can usually make an educated decision whether it is something we're looking for.

K. Kokin: I don't use readers. I read everything myself.

S. Palmer: We have purchased many scripts that have gotten "pass" coverage and passed on many scripts that have gotten "consider" coverage. Coverage only has weight in that it can encourage the executives to read a script more quickly if it gets good coverage — but if the reader slams the script, then it will take a lot longer to actually read it.

D. Friendly: Coverage is usually just a back-up for me. I would never make a determination on a script based on the coverage alone. But coverage does help us eliminate things based on concept. For example, we don't do anything that's particularly violent or exploitive. If I see a script that comes in that's based on a very violent video game, I know that's not going to be for us. We're not going to make that movie so I don't have to waste my time reading it, even if it's well-executed. That's just not what we do. That's where coverage can help with things that just aren't going to appeal to us from a genre standpoint.

S. Brooks: Coverage is helpful, but only for reading the synopsis and concept. We don't give much weight to the evaluations. We like to decide those for ourselves. We might be interested in a script with a really strong concept, but that wasn't well-executed. That script would traditionally get poor coverage — but we might still want it. Likewise, we've made TV movies from scripts with stellar concepts but bad writing. Of course, we rewrote the screenplay first.

S. Schur: Since we're a small company, I'm reading most of the material that comes in. On the occasions where I do get coverage, it can be a valuable tool for grasping the nuts and bolts of the story. You can usually tell from the synopsis whether the project is worth getting involved with.

MARK DEMPSEY (Story Analyst): When I was at Echo Lake, we took coverage very seriously and considered readers an integral part of the process. Because of that, we were very picky about the people we hired as readers and our coverage was unusually comprehensive. We made every effort to give every project a fair chance. Just because a reader hates a script doesn't mean that the script will die there. For example, the Echo Lake executives often preferred to read the coverage summaries first — without knowing what the reader's ultimate cover-page recommendation was — so that they could arrive at their own conclusions without being prejudiced by the reader's comments. That way, if a project sounded interesting, someone else would likely take a look, even if the reader had been less than enthusiastic. And in those instances when readers love something, we gave that script top priority and got someone else at the company reading it right away.

· ·

By what page do you know if something works?

K. Kokin: 30.

D. Friendly: I usually give a script up until the first act or the first 35 pages. If I haven't gotten into it by page 35, I'm usually out.

D. Stroncak: It only takes a few pages — 3 to 5 — to see if the writer has talent, but I generally need to get to the first plot point to see if the story's working for me or not.

M. Schreibman: Somewhere between page 10 and page 20.

P. Miller: Page 2. If a script doesn't grab you immediately, we don't continue. Quality writing has to grab you at the first sentence, the first page, and maintain that quality throughout.

S. Palmer: The last page.

S. Brooks: Depends on the script. But if you can't determine the concept by page 10 and if you aren't totally hooked by page 20, it's not for us. I tell my staff to give themselves until page 30 to see if it works.

S. Schur: By the "inciting incident." Around page 30, I'll know whether it has potential or is just recycling fodder.

C. Blumenthal: I usually read 40 to 50 pages of a spec script before I know if it's going to work or not. A lot of people will only read 30 pages and there are a few people out there who will only read 10 pages. I'm a little more lenient, especially if I know it's a new writer. Although the inciting incident should take place by page 15 and a twist by page 30; if it's a new writer, he or she may have all the elements but the structure may be slightly off, so I will typically keep reading until I find an interesting element or twist. But if it's not there by page 50, it's not worth my time to continue reading.

M. Dempsey: By page 40, you should have reached the first act break and gotten a clear sense of the plot and the character journeys. Scripts by that point are either working or they're not. But you can usually tell much, much sooner whether the script is a good one.

KIRA GOLDBERG (Development Executive): Not until the end of the script. But I think most executives know by page 30 if something doesn't work and that's usually enough reason to put down a script. They know their bosses won't get past that point — neither will the studio, and neither will the talent. At the end of the day, that's how movies get made.

....

What are the primary reasons for a script being rejected?

K. Kokin: Not being moved on an emotional and/or intellectual level.

D. Stroncak: Poorly executed. Not focused. Flat characterizations and on-the-nose dialogue.

D. Friendly: Generally, scripts are rejected if they're not well-written, they don't move you, or they don't have anything original to say. The ones that get you excited are the ones that have an original voice and affect your emotions — whether it's laughing or crying, they do something to you. The worst script is one that's just bland. Like, "Well, that was pretty well-written, but I was just bored to tears." That's the worst thing you can say.

M. Schreibman: It's terrible! The story is contrived and the characters are weak. This is usually the case when the script is plot-driven and not character-driven.

P. Miller: Format, genre, terrible writing, obnoxious creator, etc.

C. Blumenthal: On average, I pass on two to three scripts per day. The main reason I pass on a script is the story. Most of the scripts I read are not stories I would want to pay ten bucks to see at the theater. Novice writers most often write small, independent types of scripts. This is fine if they have an opportunity to make an independent film. But most of the time I'm looking for commercial scripts that will appeal to a larger audience. However, I have considered some wonderful scripts with little story that just contained amazing characters.

The second most popular reason I pass on scripts is because of the writing. There are a lot of poorly written scripts out there! A script can be considered poorly written if the dialogue doesn't flow, if the characters are flat, if the tone of the movie isn't apparent, and/or if the story is missing a conventional three-act structure.

S. Palmer: The vast majority of scripts that are submitted lack a strong central idea.

S. Brooks: Weak concept. Bad writing. Seen it before.

M. Dempsey: Execution and content. Poorly executed scripts are often easy to spot because of the clunky dialogue, the overwritten scene descriptions, and the murky characters. But poorly executed scripts can often be trying to tell an interesting story. Indeed, many times we've agreed to look at scripts on the basis of a compelling, fresh premise only to find that the execution is terrible. In other words, poor execution doesn't always mean that the underlying premise is bad. Conversely, there are plenty of well-executed, polished scripts out there with problematic content. "Problematic" here is obviously a judgment call. A script can be problematic for marketing reasons — say, a grim, depressing drug addict story that no one in their right mind would pay to see; familiarity reasons, yet another cookie-cutter spin on the "meet cute" romantic comedy; or reasons that have nothing to do with the script at all, like a story that's too similar to one that the company is already developing, or a script that needs more development than the production company might have the resources to commit at the time. "Problematic" just means a story that's not right for that particular executive.

There's a continuum to all of this, obviously, and few rejections are easy. One person's "problematic" script is likely another person's dream script. It's common sense, really — scripts get passed on because of either the execution of the writing or the content of the plot. You can always master execution, but there's really no way to ever predict how people will respond to the content. But all it ever takes is one person to really love it.

S. Schur: We ask ourselves if *this* is a project that Ralph Macchio would get excited about.

BUZZ WORD

Alan Smithee – A DGA-sanctioned pseudonym that a director is allowed to use in select instances when a film goes awry, having been egregiously re-cut or re-edited to the point that it no longer resembles the film that the director shot.

Which do you prefer and why — finding material on spec or developing material in-house?

D. Friendly: Well, I think you have to do both. We developed an original idea of mine called *Laws of Attraction*, from soup to nuts. We hired all the writers, shepherded the script through the entire writing process, then got the movie made with Pierce Brosnan and Julianne Moore. It's a fantastic, very creative way to produce. That is probably my favorite, most stimulating challenge of producing. But if you just rely on doing that, you wouldn't get enough movies made. So you've got to look at everything — books, pitches, treatments. You just never know where it's coming from.

M. Schreibman: Finding material on spec is much preferred. Developing material is a crapshoot at best and can take years, and sometimes goes through many transformations because of the various people involved. Spec material though, in actuality, has already been developed by the screenwriter — to the point where a producer can now start to realize it. If that means a couple of supervised rewrites to get the project from the page to the screen, then so be it.

D. Stroncak: Developing material in-house, because it allows the producer to add his voice to the project.

P. Miller: It depends on the author. Either/or.

S. Schur: Finding a great spec is like finding a winning lottery ticket. Every development executive drools at the thought of a top-notch spec finding its way into your stack, but then reality slaps you in the grill. Developing in-house material, like developing books, is a long process, but can be very rewarding when it pays off. Seeing an idea through from its inception to the screen is the ultimate in dedication and passion. However, it's also very time-consuming and is a much riskier venture.

S. Brooks: It's not a matter of "prefer" for us. We pursue each vigorously. We are always developing material in-house — primarily pitches. But because each network we pitch has very specific and unique needs, sometimes that means we'll try to find spec material, too.

S. Palmer: A truly great movie idea is such a rare commodity that it can come in any form. I think studios would option a Post-it® note if the material was strong enough.

....

How do you evaluate and balance the acquisition of book properties vs. spec screenplays?

S. Palmer: A good story is hard to find, so it doesn't really matter whether it is in a spec or book format. The expectation is that it takes longer to develop a book into a movie than a spec script, but in my experience, development can be a lengthy process no matter what the source material.

D. Stroncak: There's no preference. It always depends on whether or not we like the story, regardless if it's a book or screenplay.

P. Miller: Quite frankly, we're more interested in developing relationships with writers who write books and also have the ability to adapt their works into screenplays.

S. Brooks: On a project-by-project basis. If we love the book or spec, we pursue it. There is no predetermined balance. Since writers rarely ever write spec TV movie scripts, we tend to read features in turnaround or specs that didn't sell.

S. Schur: Book properties are usually a tougher sell and take longer to develop but are often good sources of compelling stories — it's tough to make books your bread and butter unless you're a Scott Rudin. I think in balancing material sources, a nice healthy mix of the two is always a good idea.

K. Goldberg: Books are much harder, generally speaking, because they are already a step behind having a script. Ultimately, getting a greenlight involves hiring a writer, then developing the drafts, then attaching talent, and finally getting a studio to sign on. And it's important to remember that not every good book equates to a good movie. But a book can be worth it if it provides original fodder, really great characters, or a world from which you can shape the movie.

D. Friendly: One of the advantages of a screenplay is you're that much closer to making a movie if it's good, but a book sometimes has the built-in marketing advantage if a large portion of the public is familiar with the title. But my attitude is, you can't really say, "Well, we develop this way," or, "We only do this." You gotta look at everything. Be an open book and be willing to look at everything.

••

Do you ever listen to pitches from new writers who have great sample spec scripts? If so, how did they get to you?

M. Schreibman: Yes. Anyway they can.

K. Kokin: Yes, but they have to be referred to me through someone I know.

P. Miller: Yes, occasionally. They get to me by reputation or through our Web site.

S. Brooks: Sure. We are always looking for great new talent. Almost every time we learn of the writer, it's from an agent or network executive. There is really no other way to get to us.

H. Becker: Certainly. Either they can call me or send the script to me. I might read it or I might go through a filter and have my assistant read it, but it doesn't have to come through an agent. I'm open and I'm always looking for new material.

D. Friendly: Yes, we do if an agent gets us a script and we really like it. Even if we don't want to buy the script, we would want to meet with the writer if the script is really well-written.

D. Stroncak: We have attended pitch festivals and listened to pitches, but we haven't bought anything from a pitch-fest as of yet. Other than that it's only through agents, managers, attorneys, or referrals.

S. Palmer: If I read the script and genuinely liked it, then I would consider hearing a pitch. However, it is extremely rare that we will buy a pitch, so I don't spend too much of my day listening to pitches. This has changed significantly in the past few years. It used to be much easier to get a pitch set up at a studio or bought out of a producer's discretionary fund.

C. Blumenthal: I will most definitely listen to a pitch if the writer has a good writing sample and the pitch sounds like something we'd want to develop. For me, a well-written spec script will have a unique premise, a fresh voice and entertaining characters. Pitches are very risky because you just never know what you're going to get at the end. That's why it's important to make certain the writer can create a classic three-act structure

> ### If I am going in to pitch a project, how do I prepare?
>
> The most important thing is to be prepared. Know your story, know your characters. Be quick, precise, and entertaining. I've listened to so many dull pitches that I could just about pull my hair out. For pitching, set up your characters, your plot points, and the structure of the story. Let the executives and producers know where you're at in your story and try to surprise them with original twists, turns, and an unforeseen ending. Don't take longer than fifteen minutes of their time. Good Luck!
>
> —*Chrissy Blumenthal*

and know how to tell a story from beginning to end. Also, something to keep in mind, if I read a great horror spec script and the writer wants to come in and pitch a comedy, I will most likely reject the idea because I don't know if this writer can write a comedy. If you write a great spec script and want to follow it up with a new pitch, make sure that the pitch is in the same genre. Writers can most easily get to me by sending me a query letter.

S. Schur: We're always looking for new material or ideas from writers with great sample spec scripts, regardless of whether or not they're new to the game. Any writer with a great sample is going to be repped by an

In a pitch meeting should I always start with the logline, should I compare my movie to other successful films, and should I give away my ending?

You can start with a short logline if you want, but typically if you're pitching to the studios they already know in advance what the basic premise is — if they didn't, they probably wouldn't be taking the meeting. But you should state up-front what genre your picture is, and then if you'd like, you can list a movie or two of a similar theme. I wouldn't necessarily *compare* your movie to these other successful movies but I would go ahead and compare the "tone." Often in pitches it's hard for the person hearing the pitch to understand just how the writer sees his film tonally, so this can be helpful. And if you're pitching to producers or studio executives, you *must* "give away" the ending. You want them to buy it, don't you? They won't buy a "pitch" until they know all the beats in the story — or at least all the big, important plot points, including the ending.

—*Chrissy Blumenthal*

agent, so they usually would get to us that way. Occasionally you'll find a diamond in the rough without representation, but those are few and far between.

How much time do you spend looking for new talent?

P. Miller: Every day.

S. Palmer: At least a part of every day is spent looking for new talent.

S. Brooks: Not at all. It usually has to find us. We're open to it, but as a small independent company, we don't really devote time to it.

M. Schreibman: I see new talent all the time because of my association with UCLA. I can spot excellent writers quite quickly, especially those who are good with dialogue. For me, dialogue is the key to a good script.

D. Stroncak: We like our talent to have a track record because we need something to point to when going to the studio. But still we are always

PRODUCERS, DEVELOPMENT & STUDIO EXECS

looking for writers with a unique voice — someone who stands out from the crowd and someone who has depth.

··

I can't get a producer or a development exec to read my script unless I have an agent or a manager, and I can't get an agent or manager to answer my query letter. What should I do?

S. Palmer: Pout! Actually, the people who seem to navigate the circuitous world of Hollywood most easily are people who become real students of the business. Instead of sending a generic query letter to every producer and agent in town, I recommend researching your audience and writing a specific letter to each person you want to contact. This is a lot more time consuming than sending a "Dear Sir/Madam" email, but emails with that opening line immediately cue every executive to hit the delete button before reading the email.

D. Stroncak: Write a great script and then meet as many people as you can who live and work in Los Angeles in the entertainment industry. If you live out of town, you can still go to film festivals. Everyone in LA knows *someone* and eventually cream rises to the top.

P. Miller: Unfortunately, Hollywood isn't always about what you know, but who you know. Persistence is a necessary attribute. Quality writing will prevail. Stay calm. Stay focused. And don't stop writing.

S. Brooks: Keep trying. Our business is about being able to handle rejection and continuing to pursue your dreams. If you have great material, eventually someone will notice. But you have to be resilient and keep getting up off the canvas after getting knocked down. And don't be afraid to network with friends. If someone you know has an agent, get them to recommend your work to their representation. Lots of clients are signed by word of mouth.

S. Palmer: Read the *The Hollywood Reporter* and *Daily Variety* — online subscriptions are available if you don't live in LA or NYC — to keep up-to-date on the kind of material that is selling and to whom. A wealth of information can be gleaned from the trades — new production deals, new

105

hires, new agents and managers setting up shop...and who are often look-ing for new, saleable clients. Often, in the articles or in magazine inter-views, actors will mention the kind of project they want to do next. If you have a script that fits what they describe, send a personalized note that acknowledges their specific need. This certainly won't work every time, but I know that I pay more attention when someone has taken the time to research my projects than when they just send material in blindly.

M. Dempsey: That's the $1 million question, isn't it? You somehow have to break through that wall and find someone who will read your script and then vouch for you. Networking is *crucial*. You may not know an agent or manager, but someone you know might. The more people you meet, the better your odds.

Should writers think about the budget when writing a spec script?

P. Miller: Absolutely. Particularly if they are novices.

S. Brooks: Not in my opinion. They should write what they know and be passionate about the subject. The specs that work are the ones where the reader is taken on a journey to a place they've never been before. You can tell when writers love their material and love their characters. That's what we look for, in addition to a killer concept.

D. Friendly: I would say that a new writer probably shouldn't try to write a script that takes place entirely on the water or is set in the winter. Those kinds of elements can work against the script if it looks like it's too ambi-tious an idea or too expensive. That project might get sold if David Mamet wrote it, but it probably won't from an unheard-of new screen-writer. So for starting writers, pick something a little less extravagant, so you can eliminate budget as a reason for passing.

H. Becker: I assume if a writer is writing a spec script it's because he comes to it with a real passion for the material, and that should be his only motivation. I think if he starts worrying about how much this or that is going to cost, it will affect his creative work. A writer shouldn't be influenced by the commercial aspects of a script or the perceived market-place for it, since nobody really knows what is going to sell or not. Write your own stories and don't listen to anybody else.

M. Schreibman: They should, but they don't. Writers never think of the budget when they are writing because most writers have little or no concept of what it takes to produce a movie.

M. Dempsey: If you're an unknown writer, why limit your options by writing an expensive sci-fi or disaster movie that only a studio could afford to make? Why not write a small story that could be done cheaply by an indie company? Small stories, remember, can always be pumped up and made bigger by a studio.

D. Stroncak: Absolutely. Someone has to pay for it.

....

Should a writer ever try to submit a spec script directly to a studio? Why or why not? Would you ever look at a spec that didn't come in through a known source?

S. Palmer: Studios are not allowed to accept any unsolicited material. They require that all material be submitted through a known agent in order to protect the studio *and* the writer. While working at a studio, I can't read any unsolicited scripts, but there are production companies and producers who will read query letters and scripts if they are interested in the concept.

D. Stroncak: We have a strict policy of only reading material from known sources. A writer should use referrals to get to production companies, and never go directly to the studio because they — the studios — already have deals with production companies on the lot that they are obligated to fill.

M. Schreibman: It is impossible to deliver a spec script directly to a studio, since studios only accept material from agents, managers, or attorneys. That way they are protected should there be any question of stealing or authorship. The Writers Guild also recommends that submissions be made only through appropriate sources. However, it may be possible to submit material to independent producers who have relationships with studios, and who might have a bit more leeway about accepting spec scripts. But the best way to get your work to those who can make it is still through established relationships.

S. Brooks: The question for the TV movie business would be whether or not a writer should submit a spec script directly to a network's in-house production division. I would not suggest it. The TV movie business is predominantly supplied by independent companies. They have the expertise and experience. You will get a better deal, have a better chance of getting your project made, and enjoy more creative freedom with a production company than you will with the in-house network production entity. We don't accept unsolicited material, but we do have an e-mail address where we review unsolicited concept submissions (one sentence preferred) and short synopses — if we are interested we will contact the writer.

P. Miller: I wouldn't recommend submitting directly to a studio because protocol in the industry suggests that writers be represented. But we would look at any presentation in any form. For us, it's always about the quality.

....

With the huge growth of screenplay contests, how important is winning a screenplay competition in deciding to evaluate or buy a spec screenplay?

S. Brooks: Not at all. We judge scripts on their own merit. Awards mean nothing to us.

D. Friendly: Winning a screenplay contest is okay. I don't think it can hurt to have a prize behind your screenplay, but I don't think it's that important for us. We're going to review material on our own terms.

P. Miller: It has no value in terms of our determining the worth of a project in the domestic or global markets.

PRODUCERS, DEVELOPMENT & STUDIO EXECS •

D. Stroncak: A contest does validate a script, but only if it's won a recognized contest and not one of the many unknown ones springing up weekly.

M. Dempsey: Unless you win one of the high profile, truly competitive contests — Austin, the Nicholl, Slamdance — it doesn't mean much. Those bigger contests do carry some clout, as do internal awards given by big film schools like NYU, UCLA, USC, and AFI. But there are just too many small, obscure contests out there muddying the waters. That was something we learned the hard way at Echo Lake. Too many times we'd request a script that had a laundry list of obscure screenplay contest wins, only to be disappointed.

S. Palmer: Winning a prestigious contest can certainly help the writer get attention and perhaps representation from a higher-level agent, but it doesn't make any difference as far as whether we buy the script.

....

When you receive and review material you think is great, what are the next steps toward getting the property produced?

S. Schur: I call up the studio execs right away and say, "I have your next blockbuster on my hands." If material is great, there will be a bidding war and hopefully a nice raise for me. Great material doesn't need attachments, it just needs a check written to take it off the table. Then you can have your pick of A-List writers and directors who will be knocking down your door to be involved.

S. Brooks: We option it and then determine how and where to pitch it. Each project is going to be different and require its own strategy. Sometimes we will package something with a star and sometimes we'll just go out and set up pitch meetings.

D. Friendly: If you hear a pitch or you read a script that you like, you've got to beat out the competition if anybody else is trying to develop the same material. So the first thing you have to do is get a deal done that lets the rest of the community know that *this* is *your* property. An example of that is a pitch we heard for a movie called *Don't Send Help*. We heard the pitch around two o'clock, and made the deal that afternoon by five. For us, that wasn't hard. As a company that develops our own material, we have an advantage in that we don't have as many layers of bureaucracy as a studio. If my partner, Marc Turtletaub, and I decide we want to buy something — we buy it. Any producer will tell you that one of the most frustrating things about this business is dealing with the layers of bureaucracy at the studios, which is how you sometimes lose material if you can't move quickly and aggressively enough. There are always a lot of people out there competing for good material, and there's just not that much good stuff that comes along, so when something does, you have to decide pretty quickly if you like it and then make a move for it.

D. Stroncak: If everyone agrees that it's great, then we generally would do an option with the writer through the agent. From that point we'd either get a rewrite, or, if it's already in good shape — which is rare — we would take it straight to the studio.

S. Palmer: I remember very clearly the night that I read the spec script *The Brothers Grimm* by Ehren Kruger. The producer slipped me the script the night before it went out to the rest of the town and from the moment I opened the first page, I just knew this was unlike any story I had ever read. I whipped through the script and spent the night dreaming about the characters and thinking about the best strategy to get my boss (the president of the studio) to buy the script for me.

I got into work early the next morning and waited outside my boss' office for him to arrive. The second he arrived I started my campaign about why this script was special and we needed to buy it — even though it was not the kind of material we were looking for because it was period, would be very expensive to produce, and would require a lot of special effects.

Normally, I would ask a couple of the senior executives to read the script and hope that they would agree that this was a project we should acquire. That day though, all of the senior executives were in London, so I was on my own and no one else at the company had read the script. I researched comparable movies and how much money they had made at the box office, how well-known the real Brothers Grimm were internationally, and came up with some ideas about how we could sell the movie.

I followed my boss to his car at lunchtime and jumped up and down and pitched my heart out and drummed up enthusiasm for why we shouldn't let this opportunity pass us by. Happily, in the end, we bought and developed the script. The script had more than its fair share of "Development Hell" moments where I thought it would never actually be made, but I am happy to report that the movie is now in production, starring Matt Damon and Heath Ledger.

P. Miller: First we sign a management agreement with the author, then we come up with a hit list of where we want to send the material, and *then* we get down on our knees and pray.

••

What if you love a script, but the "Powers That Be" at your company do not?

S. Palmer: I am very lucky to work at a place where I have been able to buy the majority of the scripts I have loved. Of course, a number of times I've fallen in love with the writing, but the script hasn't been the kind of movie we were looking to make in terms of subject matter. In that case, I try to meet with the writer and read other material they have written, then send the script to my friends at other studios and production companies who might be a better match for the material.

D. Stroncak: We all have pet projects and eventually we find homes for them, so I guess the answer is that we never give up when we find something we like.

P. Miller: We pass.

M. Schreibman: If your company passes and you are in a position to personally take on a project, you may want to option the project for yourself.

S. Schur: If I love a script but my superiors don't, I quickly change my tune and declare, "You're absolutely right, I didn't really like it either. I was just testing you."

Really, if there is no internal consensus on something that I think is a good script, I *will* have to pass on it because it's ultimately not my call to make. I will certainly lobby for something and convey the reasons why I love it and try to persuade my boss to see the light. If that fails, I'll definitely set up a meeting with the writer in an effort to try to work together on another project in the future.

K. Goldberg: Generally I do two things. First, I meet with the writer immediately so I can try to find an idea for them to develop that the "Powers That Be" *will* like. Second, I tell everyone I know how great the script is. There is no greater validation than seeing a script you championed get purchased and made by someone, even if it's not you. Not only will the writer appreciate your support, but so will his or her representation. Someday, when you move to the next company, you can preserve that relationship and cultivate it for the next big script. I *do* believe that every good script gets purchased at some point.

S. Brooks: I *am* the "Powers That Be." When employees at my company have passion for material, we usually try to pursue it one way or the other. In a small company we all get one or two personal projects to shepherd.

. . . .

Tell us about your relationship with a studio or studio head once they agree to develop one of the properties you have brought to them?

K. Kokin: It is total collaboration. We both need to understand the needs of the other and work towards making the best film possible.

P. Miller: You want to stay as friendly and close to that executive as humanly possible and hope that he or she keeps that job.

S. Schur: They cut us out of the loop and water the project down to the lowest common denominator whereby any chimp with an Etch-A-Sketch® could make the movie.

If you buy an article or book or life rights, how do you decide which writer to hire?

P. Miller: Oftentimes it's who the studio will accept, unless we're funding it with our own war chest. At that point, we make a decision about which author we'll put forward, because nothing is worse than putting all of this effort into a project and then hearing a response that they *would* have been interested if "so-and-so" had written it.

K. Kokin: First I call studio executives to see if they like the idea behind the article. If they do, then I have a group of writers who I usually work with and I pick the one who best responds to the material.

D. Stroncak: Agents will give us suggestions, and we're always reading writing samples, so we have a good idea of whom we want to work with before we buy a property.

S. Schur: Once the rights are secure, I'll make a list of writers whose sensibilities and track records would make sense for the type of project we're dealing with, and go over that internally until we decide on a few key names we want to pursue. At that point we'll contact the writer's agent or manager and run the idea by them. Or, if we have a personal relationship with the writer, we may go directly to him or her with the idea. Then you just whittle down the list until you find the writer who connects with the material the most.

S. Brooks: If we sell it to a network, it's a collaborative decision with them. We draw up a list of writers we have worked with before or whose material we have admired for the specific genre. Often we will be exposing the network to new ideas, and vice versa. We usually narrow it down to three or four writers and then everyone will read a sample. After that we have a discussion to decide on the order in which we'll make offers, since we don't always get our first choice.

BUZZ WORD

Biopic – A *Variety* coinage meaning biographical film: *"Coal Miner's Daughter,* about Loretta Lynn, is one of the most sucessful biopics ever produced."

S. Palmer: After buying the rights to the *New York Times'* bestseller *Bringing Down the House: The True Story of Six M.I.T. Students Who Took Vegas For Millions* by Ben Mezrich, I heard takes from eight or nine writers who all pitched their version of what the move should be. Unlike most open writing assignments — where I call literary agents and ask them to send the material to their clients — for this project, there was an onslaught of *incoming* calls. The book was excerpted in *Wired* magazine before it was published and has been incredibly popular, so a number of writers had read the book or had heard about the story before it was an open writing assignment.

We heard takes on how to adapt the book from up-and-coming writers without any produced credits, to very successful screenwriters, and some TV writers too. In the end, we hired Peter Steinfeld to adapt the book because we really responded to his take on the translation of the material to the screen. He had some very inventive ideas about how to tell the story and we had already worked with him successfully on *Be Cool*, the sequel to *Get Shorty*.

M. Schreibman: I try to find a writer who has the right sensibility for the project and one who has a track record that would appeal to either finance people or studios. The writer can be one of the key elements of a package that gets a project financed.

....

With regard to developing for television, do you have to exclusively hire writers who are approved by the networks?

P. Miller: Absolutely. Unless it's an extraordinary spec script or there's a specific reason for a network to want to produce a story, regardless of the writer.

S. Brooks: Definitely not. I've never had the network give us a list or insist on any "approved" writer.

D. Stroncak: It's important to the network that the writer on the project be on the "studio approved" list because they want to be sure that the writer can execute the script if they like the story.

M. Schreibman: It helps to have writers who are known commodities for television — television is pretty much writer-driven, as most of the producers and showrunners are writers. They are often more important than the producer or the director, and since the network requires the assurances that the project will adhere to certain guidelines, they look to known writers.

· ·

What is the process of script notes and how do you work with writers?

S. Schur: The process of script notes varies from project to project and writer to writer, but the general formula is as follows: The writer turns in a script and we do notes on it and then give it back to the writer to fix. The writer will in turn resist all suggestions and hold onto their myopic vision with a death grip.

That's what you'll hear. In reality, it's a collaborative process whereby, as the producers, we try to help the writer craft the best possible script. The hope is that each set of notes is smaller and smaller until the script has reached its full potential.

S. Brooks: It's pretty simple. We read the script and do a set of general notes as well as specific page notes. Then we call in the writer and walk him through the script page by page. He will also leave with a written copy of the notes for himself.

C. Blumenthal: Every studio and every producer has a different way of doing script notes. Typically though, once a script is acquired, the business of "re-writing" gets underway. Here, whomever is spearheading the project will do the first round of notes with the writer, taking in consideration some of the company's main concerns about the script. Normally, my script note process is quite informal: I usually read the script several times and then I write my notes directly in my script. I then meet with the writer either in person or on the phone and go page by page, giving the writer my notes. On occasion, I will just hand the script to the writer so he or she can see all my notes. When I feel that the script is in a good place — or we've run out of writing steps in the contract — I will then give it to the entire group to get a "fresh set of eyes." At that time, we'll decide if the script is worth moving forward on — i.e., giving it to talent, or the studio, or perhaps negotiating another rewrite. If we decide to give the writer "general notes" from the entire company, we meet as a group, decide which direction we want to go in, and then someone will type up the notes and present them to the writer.

M. Schreibman: I give writers the opportunity to totally exercise their own creativity. However, they also have to work within the constructs of the story being developed. On a studio project I produced, based upon a well-known novel, the writer was given the book and told to write the screenplay based upon it and to include some of the book's dialogue in the script. When he returned with the first draft six weeks later, the screenplay bore little resemblance to the novel; characters were altered and merged into other characters and the dialogue was stilted and not as witty as that in the original. I met with the writer and quietly asked, "So, did you get this out of your system?" He smiled at me, knowing what I was talking about, and nodded his head sheepishly. Then I handed him another copy of the novel and said, "Now go back and write what is in the book because *that* is what we sold to the studio." Writers must be respected, but they also need to take your notes to heart.

S. Palmer: Script notes can be a very productive, or very painful, process depending on your point of view. Basically, we give the notes that we believe will make the script better and increase its chances of being produced.

....

What is Development Hell and why do so many scripts end up there? Are there any solutions to Development Hell?

P. Miller: Development Hell is when you set your project up with a studio executive who then gets fired or leaves. The project gets passed to the next person in that position, or someone else completely, then *that* person leaves the position or is replaced, and so on and so forth. The problem is, one studio regime may acquire a property with great passion, but the next second, there's no one left who loves it.

S. Palmer: Development Hell is what happens when a script gets stuck "in development" and isn't moving forward to production. There are myriad reasons why scripts end up in Development Hell: executives who championed the project switch companies; a movie with a similar subject tanks at the box office; the budget is too high; the "Powers That Be" lose interest in the concept; an actor or director changes his or her mind or isn't available at the time the studio wants to make the movie. A project can languish in Development Hell for *years*, and it can be frustrating for everyone involved — including the studio executives — so if you come up with a solution to Development Hell, please let me know!

D. Friendly: Development Hell is when a good idea sits for too long, so nothing happens with it and sometimes it winds up never getting made. I don't know what can be done to prevent it because each project has its own course. For example, I know that *Friday Night Lights* took a long time. I was there when we bought the project, and that was over ten years ago — only now is it finally being realized. So good projects *do* get made, but it can take years. We have other projects we've been working on for five or six years at least. The only way to get out of Development Hell is to find somebody who has a passion and a vision for your material or your idea. Great producers — all the great producers, throughout the history of the movie business — do not give up. They are relentless and passionate about their material, and they keep fighting to get it made.

S. Brooks: Development Hell is when a script loses momentum at a network and gets stuck going nowhere. All projects have their own trajectories. When you first sell it, every project has the greatest of expectations. If the first draft doesn't meet those expectations, the excitement starts to dissipate. It's hard to rejuvenate that excitement. The best way to avoid Development Hell is to spend a great deal of time, and work, on the first draft. You only get one chance to make a first impression. We want to be sure that the first draft is *dazzling*. That's our best defense against failed expectations.

D. Stroncak: Development Hell does exist and it's generally because too many people are involved in a project and they all have different visions for it. Also, many times — but not always — a script is purchased because it's high-concept, but then it's incredibly difficult to develop into a coherent story that works on the screen.

S. Schur: Development Hell is when a project is stuck in the development process and isn't reaching its full potential. The causes of this Hell can vary, but often, conflicting ideas between the producers, writers, and studio can lead to simple stagnation. Also, sometimes the story just can't be cracked to the satisfaction of everyone involved. Projects can be in limbo for years, causing loss of hair and sanity for everyone involved. Usually the only way to get out of Development Hell is to set the script aflame and giggle incoherently.

M. Schreibman: Development Hell is what happens when too many people are involved in the development process. I believe it is a waste of time. If you are going to make a film, make it. Don't dawdle and continually work and rework a project before deciding to do it.

C. Blumenthal: On my first day as a development executive, my boss walked into my office and placed a gold plaque on my desk. It read simply, "Development Hell." As he turned around, he proudly announced, "Welcome to it." I later learned that *his* boss, and now partner, had passed the plaque down to *him* and he just couldn't wait to pass it on to me. I have since learned the true meaning of Development Hell.

What is Development Hell? Picture a tornado — like the kind from *The Wizard of Oz*. The tornado is our "project." In the center of the tornado, picture a script, and for all intents of purposes it's a good script. Next to the script is a stubborn writer, a pushy producer, a narcissistic director, a know-it-all studio-head, a demanding actor, and a busy actress — not that any of these people really exist, of course. Back to the tornado. The tornado goes around and around, never finding satisfaction and wreaking havoc at every turn. The twister may drop an actor here or there and pick another one up there along its way. The new actor demands that the writer re-write his part — it's not big enough, dark enough, funny enough, whatever. The producer doesn't like the new rewrite and fires the writer. So the tornado picks up another writer along the way and guess what? The director removes himself from the storm citing differences in creative direction. The actress is upset now because the director is M.I.A., so she decides to find another cyclone to ride. The

studio '
after ⁊
age
N⁾

n the whole thing, but only
ands of dollars worth of dam-
a new town/studio to destroy.
k home! Oz/Hollywood can be a

....
et rewritten?

dialogue sucks and the material as written
to the project.

merous reasons, but the most common is that
u.   ver on the concept. It is less common on television
movies,   cts where we *have* used a second writer, it was only
after several u.   had been done with the first writer and more work still
needed to be done.

D. Stroncak: Because writing for the screen is a collaborative business.
The filmmaker has his vision, the producer has the story he or she is trying to tell, and the studio has to meet its needs as well. It's the nature of
the beast.

....
*Why do so few movies get made as compared to how many are
developed?*

D. Friendly: I think it's really hard to develop a good script, number one.
And when you do develop a good script, all the stars have to line up in
the heavens for somebody to actually want to make your movie. One of
the difficult realities about the film business is that it's not a meritocra-
cy. The best scripts don't simply rise to the top and get made. Every year
there are articles about the ten best scripts that were never made. There's
a kind of a mystery to what gets made and what doesn't, and it's an
impossible thing to analyze. Not only do you have to be talented, but the
planets have to line up. That sounds a little spiritual, but there's a lot of
luck involved. Talent isn't enough — you have to be talented *and* lucky.

S. Palmer: Movies are an incredibly expensive business; studios will often research and develop a number of ideas simultaneously rather than put all their eggs in one basket.

D. Stroncak: There are a number of reasons, but basically everyone has different taste. If a new head of development is hired, he'll probably start looking for new material and put all the old stuff on the back burner so he can find projects that make him shine rather than projects that make his predecessor look good.

K. Kokin: There aren't enough stars and directors with the clout to generate the financing for the number of scripts out there.

P. Miller: Books cost thousands of dollars, movies cost millions of dollars. The key to successful motion picture production is distribution. Many independent films never see the light of day because they never get distribution.

S. Brooks: There is less development in television movies. At broadcast networks the development to production ratio tends to be around three to one. At cable networks it can get down to two to one, or even less. We've made movies at two basic cable networks where their development to production ratio is around one-and-a-half to one. The feature business is a *whole* different animal.

BUZZ WORD

Blind script deal – When the network or studio gives a writer a script deal before they know what the idea is for the script. The term "blind script deals" (a.k.a. "blind script commitments") almost exclusively applies to those writers with a track record. Such writers often have several active projects at once and studios, networks, and larger production companies will make a blind script deal in order to guarantee they'll have a project with that writer. Sometimes, a buyer will make a blind script deal as part of a deal to purchase a hot (or great) script. By the way, from what I've seen, the deals aren't wholly "blind," i.e., the writer must pitch the idea that he or she is going to use to fill the commitment, and the network (studio, etc.) must sign off on it. Of course, there's a reason that the writer earned the blind script deal in the first place, and so the network or studio is often very motivated to get that writer working on a script for them.

—Grady Hall

S. Schur: Getting a movie made is one of the hardest things on the planet to do. There are so many things that can go wrong that can kill a project. The stars really have to be aligned for a movie to get made. Sometimes studios will buy a project just to kill it, because it's too similar to something else they're developing. Sometimes the development process goes haywire and nobody can figure out how to crack the story or solve its problems. Sometimes you can't get an attachment that would be meaningful enough for a studio to want to make it. It's really a miracle that any movie gets made.

....

Beyond the big talent agencies, how much business do you negotiate with legitimate boutique literary agencies? What kind of material and what sort of writers do you seek from these companies?

D. Friendly: We talk to everybody. Obviously, we just don't know where the good material is coming from, and it would be a mistake to ignore the smaller agents. We try to cover all of them. Obviously, we deal more frequently with the bigger agencies, but some of the real gems come out of the smaller places. You have to have relationships with everybody, and you cannot have enemies. One way to avoid making enemies is to respond quickly. I don't think people mind getting a "pass," but they don't want to be hung out to dry.

S. Brooks: We do just as much business with the quality boutique agencies as we do with the five majors. We look for good concepts and good scripts wherever we go. Because the TV movie business is not something vigorously pursued by the major agencies, there are terrific writers and material at the smaller agencies.

S. Schur: Boutique agencies usually have the quirkier, more character-driven writers who might be right for a smaller, more indie-feeling project. We do most of our business with the larger agencies, but the boutiques often represent talented writers who are just waiting to pop, so it's important to keep those relationships going.

What is the most unusual thing you've ever seen/had a writer demand in a contract?

D. Stroncak: That the writer be attached to direct and/or act in the film even though they're unproduced and have never directed or acted in a major feature film before.

M. Schreibman: I once had a writer demand that he be left alone without any script notes or interference of any kind for two months. He also required a constant supply of jellybeans, making sure that the contract reflected that he receive a two pound box of Jelly Bellies® every week he was working. Go figure....

P. Miller: A participation in the gross profits on a studio picture, and that the writer direct and star in it, too.

S. Palmer: Truthfully, writers' contracts are not nearly as ludicrous as actor's demands often are — but I did once have an A-list writer try to convince me that the studio should reimburse him for his purchase of a $600 pair of handmade Italian leather shoes!

S. Brooks: Writers are so rarely demanding about anything. They are usually so appreciative to get the job and be able to write for a living — most would be happy to write for free. But I do remember one writer who insisted that when he flew to a location in Europe it was on an airplane with four engines on the wings, not two. We thought that was pretty unusual.

Do you want writers to keep in touch with you?

S. Brooks: Absolutely. And they do. We work with the same writers over and over. On occasion they will send us ideas or pitch us new stories or scripts. We are all storytellers. We treasure our writer relationships more than any other.

S. Palmer: It's always nice to get a call or an email from writers I have worked with before to let me know that they've finished their next spec script or are pitching a new project and would like me to consider it.

K. Goldberg: It would really depend on the writer and whether I responded to their material. I think the best route is email. That way executives can respond to writers when they have a chance. Be careful to remember that executives are juggling their own bosses, the studio, other writers, multiple projects, and submissions — so try not to harass them. Give them a chance to respond and let them make efforts to show their level of interest.

S. Schur: Only if they're talented...or they specialize in Ralph Macchio period epics.

ASK THE PROS

READERS/STORY EDITORS

What percentage of the scripts you read move up the ladder to the next stage? How often do you "recommend"?

RIO HERNANDEZ: In the ten or so years that I have been reading scripts, I would say it has been very rare that I have recommended a script and seen it "moved up the ladder." The primary reason for this is that any "hot" script, or one penned by a professional, working writer, will generally be read by one of the development executives or the producer rather than going through the reader process. There are exceptions, of course. When I read for a company that accepted unsolicited scripts, they were looking to discover new talent so I flagged several scripts that stood out as having potential. Another exception is work submitted as a writing sample by an agent. In this case the reader is being called upon to note the quality of the writing itself, in those cases, I would be more likely to suggest that the executives take a look at the material. It certainly behooves a reader to be very serious when it comes to recommending a script, as your recommendation means that an executive or producer will take time to read the material. Executives have huge reading loads already, and it's not always possible to for them to read every script in its entirety. So you want to really feel that something is an exceptional piece of writing or has a great concept and warrants serious attention. The people you read for place a good deal of trust in you and you're essentially putting your own reputation on the line when you give a piece of writing a recommend.

LISA CRON: I have read scripts and manuscripts at varying stages of completion and studio involvement, so it's impossible to say what percentage actually move up the ladder because many are already several rungs up when I read them. If I absolutely had to put a number to it — and this isn't scripts that get made, but scripts and manuscripts that start at square one and get further consideration — I'd say it's somewhere around 5 percent. I rarely recommend, but when I do, I do it with utter gusto. I want writers to succeed. I *want* to be swept away. This is one of the reasons the first few pages are so important. If you pull readers into your world early on, they're much more likely to accept things that might be seen as red flags in other, less compelling, scripts. Also, to clarify, most studios and production companies have a category between "recommend" and "pass," known as "consider" or "maybe" — one major studio even had a fourth category called "no — see comment" which meant that ultimately the script was a pass, but there was some mitigating element that was worth a second look. So, while rare, there is the possibility of moving up the ladder from a consider rather than a flat-out recommend.

....

By what page do you know if something works?

R. Hernandez: I honestly don't think you can say what "works" until you have read the whole thing. Sure, you'll notice superb writing on page one — but the script could fall apart in the end. Something that might have mediocre writing may have such a great plot or twist that you'd want to recommend it if only for the concept. That said, I have read scripts where the level of writing was so amateur that I knew, almost immediately, that it was never going to amount to anything. Fundamentals like characters and a story are generally considered required, but I have read scripts without these, amazing as that might seem. If I'm reading a script and I feel like the writer has no idea what they're doing, I'll become impatient and probably be more critical. Still, as a reader, I have to finish everything I'm hired to read. Obviously, studio executives and agents don't have this

Things to Remember... Things to Avoid

Here is a list, in no particular order, of content errors that can quickly derail what sounded like such a fresh concept when you first thought of it:

- The hero doesn't have anything at risk. We need to know what "doing the right thing" will cost the hero. The same holds true for every other character — each character *must* have something at risk. The flip side is that each character has to want something — which, of course, is what they hope to gain by putting something they already have at risk. There is no truer maxim than the old reliable: Nothing ventured, nothing gained.

- There *is* dramatic tension, but it doesn't build. Often this is because the stakes don't mount with each successive scene. Instead, the same scene is simply rewritten over and over until the climax. Each successive scene *must* move the story forward.

- The characters are too familiar. Up to a point, familiar is good, because it makes the audience feel at home — these are people they know. As the screenwriter, your job is

➡

mandate, so they may be able to better say when they will or won't continue reading a script.

L. Cron: That depends on what you mean by "works," which is often a relative question. The short answer is a non-answer: It varies script by script. A similar but far more crucial question is, when do you know what the script is about? The answer, in a good script, is "almost immediately." If you don't have some idea what the story is about in the first few pages, chances are you never will. I can't tell you how many scripts I've read where the only accurate answer to the question, "What is it about?" is, "It's *about* 120 pages." This isn't to say that the entire story has to be obvious by page three, just that there has to be enough dramatic tension to make the reader want to know what happens next. There is no exception to this rule. It doesn't matter how well-written, how fully realized the characters, or how timely the concept — without dramatic tension, it will be an automatic pass.

As for if it ultimately "works," scripts are so often re-written once optioned, it's impossible to say if it works — meaning, will it be recommended — until I've read it entirely. Sometimes I'll read something, sure I'm going to pass on it, and then the last act is so strong that I find myself doing an about-face. Which is frustrating, because chances are good that by then I've already written a wonderfully scathing critique in my head, which now has to be scrapped. The much more common scenario, however, is that a script starts with great promise and just never comes close to fulfilling its potential. This is because it is so much easier to write setups than it is to pay them off. To further complicate things, everything that happens in the first act will read as if it's a setup and so readers will begin spinning possible scenarios from the get-go. When these apparent plot points turn out to be irrelevant, they aren't forgotten — instead, the reader uses them as nails in the script's coffin.

Finally, while I read every script to the bitter end, the sad truth is that the vast majority are so poorly written that it is quite clear from page one that there will nothing there to recommend. Often the most entertaining part of reading is picking up ammunition for the biting critique you're going to write when you finally, mercifully, reach "Fade Out".

What are the primary reasons for a script being rejected?

R. Hernandez: This is a *much* easier question to answer. The first thing you look for is exceptional writing and/or a great concept. Without either of these qualities, the script will be a

to give these familiar characters a fresh twist. Familiarity gives us a frame of reference, so when the characters do something unexpected, we are genuinely surprised. In other words, you've allowed a character we thought we knew inside and out to grow, and that is what makes the character compelling. But without a fresh twist, no matter how well-written, familiar characters come across as stale and stereotypical.

- Way too much detailed stage direction. To be told your stage direction is novelistic is *not* a compliment. Stage direction should be as short as possible, with nothing superfluous. Remember: Less is more. Always. Also (ideally), your audience isn't reading the film — if your stage directions aren't visual, your audience cannot know what they are. It's amazing how many writers will give their character's backstory in the stage direction. For instance, from an actual script: "DOCTOR BONEAPART, a sadistic physician, lost his license years ago for experimenting on live human beings." How on earth does an actor portray all that onscreen?

➡

- The subplots don't reflect, mirror, or impact on the main storyline. A successful subplot must in some way resonate against the central story. If it doesn't, it stops the story dead. Remember, every scene must move the story forward in some way. A related peeve is a seeming setup that isn't one after all. One very important thing to keep in mind is that everything in a screenplay reads either as a setup, a payoff, or the road from one to the other. Often writers introduce a fact or character to solve a problem in that particular scene, without realizing that it sets up an expectation in the audience's mind. Everything in a screenplay impacts on everything else. This is especially true of characters and events introduced early on — the audience will expect that they will come into play later on, and feel let down if they don't.

- Anything that even faintly resembles *Deus Ex Machina* — that is, introducing a new character or fact late in the game that couldn't possibly have been intuited before, but now tidily solves the hero's main problem — is another very bad idea. Not only will ➡

pass. Another consideration is whether or not the material is suitable for the company you're reading for. Oftentimes you will have an edict as to what type of projects they want — when I read a great script that simply doesn't seem a right fit for the company, I mention that it's a great piece of work and attach the caveat that it doesn't seem to be a project they would be interested in pursuing. I think the one quality I look for most is whether or not the material is fresh or is it just a lazy rehash of other scripts. If something is unique, or has its own voice, it immediately captures my attention.

L. Cron: First, there are the reasons that have little to do with the script: a film with the exact same premise has just been released, the script is a hundred million dollar action thriller and the studio only does low budget comedies, or, the most frustrating reason of all — because the protagonist reminds the producer of his wife or her ex-husband. Of course, scripts can also move up the ladder for the very same reasons. What are the primary reasons for a script being rejected that are within the writer's control? Bad writing. No story. No conflict. No dramatic tension. No internal logic. No structure. The problem with screenwriting is that it looks easy. How hard could it be to write 120 pages, and look at all that white space!

In truth, screenwriting is one of the hardest forms to master. It's shocking how many scripts read as if they were written by people who have never actually watched movies.

There are also a gaggle of smaller offences that, when combined, can tip the scale against you. For instance, it's of utmost importance that a script be properly formatted. This isn't just because readers are sticklers for form, or even that an improperly formatted script signals that the writer is an amateur. It's that we read at warp speed, and if you deviate from the accepted format, it makes your screenplay that much harder to read. It is difficult enough to write a script that flows; it's a travesty to stop that flow with formatting that constantly pulls the reader up short. And believe me, the last thing you want to do is needlessly annoy the reader from the start.

Misspellings are irritating. Sure, most of us occasionally write "it's" when we mean "its," or make the mistake of typing "your" where we mean "you're" — when we do it, we recognize it for what it is, and it's not a big deal. But when someone else does it? What an idiot! So, since you don't want us idiots to think you're one, do your best to catch it when you've written "their" and what you really mean is "they're," and "to" instead of "two," too.

the audience feel cheated, but also you'll have totally sacrificed the internal logic of the world you've created.

- There is no genuine force of opposition. Thus, the hero has nothing to play against and he doesn't get the chance to prove his worth. Many writers love their heroes so much that they can't bear to put them into genuine peril. The trouble is, without genuine peril, he can't truly become a hero!

- There is a villain but he isn't well defined enough. Or, he doesn't do much. The villain can't be a nebulous threat that never really materializes or acts. He has to take action, and the action has to mount. His job is to put the hero to the test, preferably a test that even the hero doesn't think he can pass! Alternatively, the villain isn't *good* enough. What does this mean? No one is bad to the bone. Or, if they are, they don't see themselves that way. You must let your villain be likable — thus accessible — in some small way. The more we can relate to him as a human being, the more heinous — and compelling — his bad behavior will seem.

—*Lisa Cron*

Make sure that your screenplay isn't printed on both sides of the page. While, yes, one of the most established agencies does do this, and it is ecologically sound, it makes your script much more cumbersome to read. It breaks the flow considerably.

Make sure that none of your characters have similar names — a script with main characters named Carla, Casey, and Carrie is impossible to follow.

Please: *Never* use a picture or illustration as a cover page. Never, ever, ever. Really.

· ·

Is there a trick to getting a screenplay past a reader?

R. Hernandez: There is no trick to getting a script past a reader — except writing a really good script. That said, it's also very important to make sure your script looks professional and is properly formatted. The surest way to have your script not be taken seriously is for it to look unprofessional. Get a screenwriting program and look at produced screenplays to see how they are formatted. Most of all: no pictures on the cover, no fancy spiral binding, no colored pages, and no wacky fonts. All these things do is signal that you are not a professional and not to be taken seriously.

L. Cron: Sure: sleep with the producer. Other than that, the only thing you can do is write a fabulous screenplay. For your own sake, be absolutely sure your screenplay is ready before you send it out. You only get one chance. Get as much feedback as you can first — and not just from your friends, even friends in the business. No matter how objective they say they are or try to be, they are either giving you the benefit of the doubt, or lying. This isn't to say that your script might not be absolutely great, but you can't trust them to tell you if it's not; you need to run it past someone who knows how to read a screenplay, and ideally, someone who doesn't know you at all.

BUZZ WORD

Boffo – A *Variety* term to mean highly sucessful, usually applied to box office performance: "*My Best Friend's Wedding* has been boffo at the B.O."

Have you ever read a script that you believed in 100 percent, but it never got made?

R. Hernandez: There are a few great scripts floating around that haven't been made yet that everyone says you should read if you want to see some stellar writing. One of these scripts was *Monster's Ball*, which, of course, was finally made into a film. One that hasn't been made yet is Hossein Amini's *Shanghai*. Fortunately, pretty much every *great* script I've read has been made, which I think is a testament to the fact that great material will be recognized eventually.

L. Cron: No. But here's a story that illustrates the workings of the game that have nothing to do with the quality of the material. I was reading for a major production company, and — an anomaly — had recently read several scripts I'd liked, when I was assigned a children's book that had already been published. I'd never heard of it, but my son and his friends had. When I asked them about it, they sat me down and breathlessly gave me a glowing in-depth synopsis of the book — one worthy of the most accomplished story analyst. Quite honestly, I wasn't as enamored of the novel myself, but wrote a very positive recommendation nonetheless. When I turned it in, the head of the story department called me, annoyed, and said, "Lisa, you know you don't have to like *everything*." The book was *Harry Potter and the Sorcerer's Stone*.

Have you ever rejected a script and then seen it go on to become a hit movie?

R. Hernandez: No, never.

L. Cron: No. But here's another story that illustrates the gray area. I covered, in manuscript, a comic novel then titled *Father Figure*. I absolutely loved it. But I was reading for a major studio and felt that, it being a small, character-driven British comedy, it wasn't for them. I passed with a "no — see comment." A few weeks later, the book was picked up by a small but prestigious production company, and went on to become *About A Boy*.

....

How do you objectively read a certain genre if your taste and passion is in a different direction?

R. Hernandez: I think that no matter what your personal taste is you have to be able to recognize a film that succeeds on its own terms and a script that is good no matter what the genre. I also think it's important to see a wide range of films so you have a reference for what makes a great comedy, a great action film, a great romantic comedy, and so forth. I also think that a great concept will always stand out and that strong writing will always shine. Of course, there are going to be those occasions where you might run up against something that is just not your cup of tea, or you might be blind to what someone else might see in it. I try to keep my critique to an analysis of the work's strengths and weaknesses and try not to focus on whether or not it's the type of film I might personally rush out to see.

L. Cron: It's easy. Readers must have a highly developed sense of story, structure, pacing, and character development — all of which are the fundamental elements of any script or novel. This, then, is the primary yardstick by which scripts are initially judged in terms of viability. The genre — what the story is actually about — is practically irrelevant. The sad truth is that most scripts do not survive this preliminary round of scrutiny. For those scripts that do make the first cut, readers must be familiar with every genre — regardless their own personal taste — so they know what's been done, what's fresh, what's hot, and any other idiosyncrasy or peculiarity playing well at the box office. For instance, I just read drop-dead fabulous horror manuscript — it was evocative, visceral, and extremely visual. While I would rarely go to horror movie by personal choice, I do make it my business to see just about everything. Which is why my heart sank as I read further into the manuscript. It was about a woman with supernatural powers who is hired to keep a war between vampires and werewolves from beginning. In short, *Underworld*, which had just opened.

But of course, it would be naive to say that personal taste can be totally eradicated, regardless your best efforts to do so. I'd have to say, however, that a reader far is more likely to err in the direction of what

they love — that is, giving something a better than deserved recommendation — than in rejecting a great script in a genre they don't personally like. Here's why: There are so few really great scripts out there, that
when you actually read a fabulous one, you get so excited that it never
occurs to you to reject it, no matter what it's about.

....

How did you get to become a reader? What are the attributes of
a good reader? How many scripts do you read a week on the
average?

R. Hernandez: I started working as a reader in New York City. It's much
easier, I think, to break into reading there. I was working as an assistant
to a director and one of the producers on the film recommended me for
a reading job at the production company where she worked. I think being
around executives, producers, directors, and so forth is a good way to get
your foot in the door — it is a highly competitive market with not a lot
of great reading jobs to go around. Another great way to start is as an
intern at a production company, as most internships provide you with an
opportunity to do coverage. Then you'll have samples of your work to
show and can pursue paying jobs as a reader. To be a good reader you
should have a thorough knowledge of film as it helps to compare a script
to movies that have already been made. You should also love movies and
have a passion for what makes them great. You should be able to talk
about structure, character arcs, conflict, and so on, and be able to make
thoughtful and specific critiques. But perhaps the most essential component of being a good reader is the ability to read fast and so read a high
volume of material. When I read for a studio, I used to receive almost
more work than I could handle — several books a week and several more
scripts. But because of the volume, I was able to support myself with just
that one reading job. Most other places I've read for have given me
maybe three to six scripts a week, so I needed a couple of reading jobs to
make ends meet. As an aside, I would mention that if you are a fast reader and can plow through a 400 page book in a day or so, you have a good
chance of finding work reading books for companies. I've found there are
more opportunities if you specialize in reading books. Right now I read
an average of three books a week.

L. Cron: I started in New York back when most of the major studios had an East Coast story department. That has changed dramatically in the past six years. I had a background in publishing, and a friend who had read for years asked if I'd like to give it a try. I started out covering books and manuscripts for possible adaptation to film and/or TV. Before I started reading, I couldn't have articulated what makes a book adaptable, but I found that the minute I began reading with that in mind, it became completely obvious. I believe most of us who love movies and books have this skill, whether we know it or not. The same skill applies to reading scripts, although it's much more difficult because the form is so deceptively difficult. Almost everyone I know who reads for a living — rather than working as an assistant or in the mailroom where you're expected to read as part of the job — got into the business by networking or knowing someone in the business.

In terms of reading, when I was reading books, I'd usually cover between four and six books a week, and the pay was far better than for reading screenplays. There were times when I was covering screenplays that the production company would deliver two or three scripts by five in the evening; by nine I'd have to call the executive with a "verbal" — a quick over-the-phone analysis — then write the coverage to be turned in the next morning.

One word on writing a synopsis: Since many aspiring readers are also writers, the idea of synopsis writing can be daunting. After all, I'd say I could synopsize a 120 page script I'd written in about, oh, 125 pages. However, I can and have synopsized a one-thousand page manuscript in three pages — double-spaced. It's much, much easier than trying to boil down something you've spent months fleshing out.

. . . .

Is coverage the same for all the companies you have read for? What are some of the differences?

R. Hernandez: For production companies, my coverage has all been pretty much the same, though some companies want different lengths. I worked for one studio that wanted your coverage as long as possible and

---

BUZZ WORD

Greenlight – When a production is given the go-ahead from a studio.

I've worked for other companies that didn't want any script synopsis to go longer than a page. As mentioned before, what *is* different is often the type of material you might recommend. You should have a sense of what the company is looking for.

L. Cron: In essence it's all the same — a synopsis followed by an analysis of the script's strengths and weaknesses. Some studios and productions companies have checkmark charts where you rate the script for character, dialogue, salability, accessibility, plot, structure, and that sort of thing. Most companies have length requirements — and usually the shorter the better. Not surprisingly, I like to write a long analysis. I believe that the executive should have an accurate and detailed assessment of the scripts strengths, weaknesses, and the ways in which it could be improved. Plus, I like to mouth off.

....
Do you interact with the executives at the company?

R. Hernandez: I've had relationships with executives, and the presidents of some smaller companies. In those situations it was just the head of the company and an assistant in the office. Then I was called upon to not only read scripts, but also do script breakdowns, notes, etc. That is a rare situation. At all of my reading jobs for larger companies I've had zero contact with executives.

....
What is the most overdone concept?

R. Hernandez: That's a hard question to answer. Right now, I feel like I've read a lot of vampire scripts and it's very tough to come up with a vampire movie that hasn't been done or doesn't seem to owe a debt to Anne Rice. Serial killers and aliens also pop up with frequency. When you feel like you've seen the definitive movie of a certain genre it's tough to come across a script that you think could be better or do something new with a concept that's already been done.

L. Cron: Thrillers of all kinds. However, they are also what sells. I've read far more vanilla thrillers than anything else. Few of them stand out —

it's such a crowded field that a script has to be genuinely stellar to leap the pack.

That being said, there is a tremendous amount of serendipity involved. Writers should write what moves them, thriller or not. The final truth is: None of the rules apply if your script has That Thing. No one can teach you that. That Thing is magic. It can be a perfect scene, a subtext that resonates, a character who feels familiar enough to be inviting and yet is unique enough to thrill and surprise, it can be a setting, a scenario, a writing style, or simply something that captivates the person with the power to greenlight it.

••

Is it true that readers skip the stage direction and just read dialogue?

L. Cron: Yes and no. The truth is that when you're flying through a script, you read what jumps out at you. If the dialogue is popping and you're barreling along, you give a cursory glance at the stage direction and motor on at warp speed. So, if something is *really* important, put it in caps. Sure, they'll tell you to capitalize any sound — and this is a good idea — and all characters need to be capitalized when first introduced. But what about something we need to see, like: "He leaves a single rose on his seat"? Ordinarily you wouldn't capitalize that. But what if it's the culmination of a subplot that has run throughout the entire script, and is part of a long montage? If it's easily missed, then who cares about the rules. Capitalize it!

ASK THE PROS
DEALMAKING

ASK THE PROS

AGENTS AND MANAGERS

What's the Number One thing that attracts you to a writer or property?

MARTY BOWEN (Agent, UTA): Talent. Specifically, I am interested in the visceral response a script gives me. If it's a comedy, it should make me laugh; if it's a drama, it should move me; if it's a horror script, it should scare me. Demand for the writer is also important. Most of the business at larger agencies is in established writers — writers who have somehow made their way into the system and are beginning to build momentum, at which point an agent finds out about them and jumps on board. That's generally how it happens. The process is a bit different at smaller agencies.

WENDI NIAD (Manager, Niad Management): I look for a writer who writes. I know that sounds weird, but you'd be surprised at how many people claim to be "writers" and all they have is one script that they've been shopping for years. I want a writer who writes a script and then moves on to the next one and lets his representatives do their jobs. They also have to be easy to work with — which means: Take notes from young studio execs, many of whom have never actually had a movie made, without complaining — and be fun in the room, to be able to make the producers and studio execs actually *want* to spend time and work with them.

In terms of property, it has to be extremely well-executed and have a "commercial" appeal. Now, that doesn't necessarily mean *Dumb and Dumber* every time, because every genre has its own commercial viability. It just means that it has to appeal to a wide audience. It has to sell popcorn. It has to be able to get Middle America into theaters.

PETER MILLER (Manager, PMA Literary and Film Management): Three ingredients: big enough, fresh enough, and high quality enough.

PAT QUINN (Agent, Paradigm): The things that attract me to writers are originality and voice. I am also interested in writers who have a polished execution, which means artful structure, interlocking plots, and unique characters. I like material that makes me laugh out loud, too. When I read the script, I don't want to put it down!

NANCY RAINFORD (Manager, independant): A writer's intelligence, wit, uniqueness, verbal storytelling, and point-of-view have to compel me to want to read something they've written. It's always subjective. I go with what excites me. I don't lean toward popular — I slant more offbeat. The writer and the writing must instinctively make me *want* to work. No agent or manager is the be all or end all. And I never advocate making a career of getting an agent. Do the work, and we'll find you.

MARTI BLUMENTHAL (Agent, Writers & Artists Group International): The number one thing that attracts me to a writer or property is the individuality of the voice behind it. One of my favorite scripts was a story about the father of a dysfunctional family who had come home to die. This was not a commercial or even a unique story, but it was told with such incredible power and emotion that it was unforgettable.

I also look for someone with the ability to tell a story with a clear theme, a beginning, middle, and end, who can write sympathetic or relatable main characters, and lastly, who is professional — they show up on time to meetings, they do the work that's required, they deliver when they are supposed to, and they appreciate the business aspects of a writing career in Hollywood.

DAVID ENGEL (Producer/Manager, Circle of Confusion): The marriage of an original voice to an awareness of the commercial side of this industry.

ADAM KOLBRENNER (Manager, Foundation Management): I look for writers who can write a movie. Some people will write a concept that completely falls apart forty pages in. I look for people who are committed, but not desperate as screenwriters. It's always very obvious in that first conversation what sort of person you are dealing with. I also look for memorable characters who are real people.

JON HUDDLE (Agent, ICM): A fresh voice and a big idea.

....

What's the Number One thing that turns you off about a writer or script?

P. Miller: Bad attitude, blatant arrogance, careless grammar, spelling errors.

W. Niad: The ones who refuse to understand that this really is a *business*. They argue with you about notes instead of taking them and logically thinking about them in terms of the business of moviemaking. They become offended and take criticism personally. If you want to get your movie made, you're going to have to listen to people who have the power to make that happen.

M. Blumenthal: I hate cute "asides" to the reader in the stage directions. It either interrupts the flow of the script or it underscores the fact that the story isn't entertaining enough in its own right and can't hold a reader's interest.

P. Quinn: Writers who are bitter and angry, and who have a chip on their shoulder. Who have unrealistic expectations of what jobs they are "entitled" to. Who make long, crazy phone calls. Who have persecution complexes, including the familiar "artist as victim" scenario. Luckily *I* don't have any of this type of client!

A. Kolbrenner: The thing I hate more than anything is a new writer who wants me to "sign a release" so I don't steal their concept. Like the concept of a group of teens in a haunted house is so goddamn original.

M. Bowen: I have as strong a visceral reaction to bad writing as I do to good — the only difference is, bad writing doesn't take as much time out of my day.

....

How do you find new writers?

N. Rainford: Writers are not hard to find. They're everywhere and everyone. I *never* look for new clients. And because I know what I'm good at selling, I am also not the right manager for everyone. I consider my clients to be partners; they are always people I like — at this point in my career, life is too short to spend time with people I don't enjoy.

M. Blumenthal: There are three ways I find new writers. First is through referrals, which can come from relatives, friends, acquaintances, other clients, producers, lawyers, managers, or studio executives. The best usually come from other clients or from studio executives — other clients because they know how valuable my time is and they rarely waste it with someone who isn't at least as talented as they are, and studio executives because they want more business from my company and they know better than to send me a client who they themselves would never hire. They know I'll be calling them the next day to put that referred client to work!

The second is by seeing, hearing, or reading their work and tracking them down. One of the top clients at our agency is a writer I heard being interviewed on the radio when I was in my car. His story was so amazing I had to pull over to call the station and find out his name. Once I got his name it was easy to find him listed in the phone book.

The third is via blind submissions or query letters. This hardly ever turns out to be the best source — I don't always read them — yet once in awhile a good project does comes through. There's a big movie opening next month that was written by a writer we found through a query letter.

P. Miller: We're self-supplying in that we get hundreds of submissions from around the globe every week.

A. Kolbrenner: Mostly from referrals, which can come from producers, agents, attorneys, friends, etc. However, I never underestimate what a bouncer or bartender has to say about his friends.

W. Niad: Anywhere and everywhere. Word of mouth has always proven to be the best for me. Everyone has, or knows someone who has, a screenplay. It might even be your cousin's friend's brother's uncle!

....

Do you accept unsolicited script submissions? If so, how does someone submit to you?

W. Niad: Yes, we accept unsolicited material, but only through query letters that are faxed or emailed to us. With unsolicited material, it's the idea that draws our interest. To break in as a new writer, you need to have a really commercial, viable spec script that, if it doesn't sell, can serve as a writing sample for the open assignments at the studios.

J. Huddle: Ninety-nine percent of our submissions come through referrals.

N. Rainford: I don't accept unsolicited scripts, and you can blame that on the really bad writers out there who have gone and ruined it for the rest of you. Also, I am never actively looking for new clients, so you might not want to waste your time — if none of that manages to deter you, send a query letter via e-mail to www.agentyouragent@aol.com. I *will* read your e-mail, but that's as much as I'm willing to promise.

P. Miller: Our submission guidelines are on our website at www.pmalit-film.com.

M. Bowen: I do not accept unsolicited material.

BUZZ WORD

Prexy – In *Variety*, the title of president: "The studio has no plans to fill the prexy post in the wake of the exec's resignation."

With the huge growth of screenplay contests, how important is winning a competition in your deciding to represent a writer?

D. Engel: Not that important. A good script that wins a competition is no better than a great script that is never entered in a contest.

A. Kolbrenner: You show me a judge in a screenplay competition and I'll show you someone with an agenda. You can tell me you won the "World Finals American Script Fiesta for the Best Script *Ever*, in the History of the Universe" — but if I don't like the writing, there's little for me to do other than pass.

P. Miller: Contests have no value to me in terms of our determining the value of a project in the domestic or global markets.

W. Niad: These days there are so many contests that they really don't mean anything anymore. What writers should look for in a contest is what it can do for their careers if they win. What is First Prize? What is Second? I'm proud to say that we've put our money where our mouths are and have a contest called "Become a Hollywood Screenwriter" where the winner receives a two-day trip to Los Angeles to have back-to-back meetings with producers, studio executives, and agents. Our winners are actually introduced to the people who can hire them or buy their material. We will provide the winner with the opportunity to begin a "career" as an actual screenwriter. That, I think, should mean more than a few thousand bucks and some coverage.

M. Bowen: No, but every once in a while the Nicholl does seem to have a little weight.

M. Blumenthal: Winning anything is good. How important is winning a screenplay competition in deciding to represent a writer? The script might be read more quickly, but if it's not of the right quality the award won't make any difference. Ninety percent of what determines whether a writer gets representation is directly due to the quality of his or her writing.

P. Quinn: Winning one of the prestigious screenwriting contests and placing at the top, or near it, is meaningful to agents. But being the fifteenth finalist somewhere isn't.

....

What are your responsibilities to a writer?

M. Bowen: The primary responsibility of an agent is to handle their client's career. Under that very broad answer one of the things is obviously to make the very best deals possible, two is to help inspire them to do their best work, and three is to help them navigate their careers so they avoid as many potential pitfalls as possible.

M. Blumenthal: Our main responsibilities are: First, to promote a writer's work with passion and commitment; second, to procure work for him or her at the studios or networks; third, to negotiate the very best deal or deals possible; fourth, to create a career plan for him or her that is long term and has built in accountability on both sides; fifth, to support and guide his or her efforts through the most honest possible feedback.

N. Rainford: SIGN, SELL, SERVICE — the credo of all agents. I also feel a personal responsibility to do what I say I will do.

P. Miller: To represent them to the best of our abilities in a consistent and unrelenting manner while preventing business complications from interfering with the creative process.

J. Huddle: To build and maintain their careers, and to help them achieve their goals.

W. Niad: According to the Talent Agencies Act, to simply to advise and counsel. We prepare the writer to become a *working* writer in Hollywood. We read draft after draft after draft, giving notes, trying to get the writer and his or her script into the best possible shape to sell.

A. Kolbrenner: It's not a job search or a placement agency. I want screenwriters for film or TV who get the business and who are anxious to work for the next twenty years. I want people who are as hungry as I am about building long-lasting careers.

· ·

How closely do you work with writers on their material?

J. Huddle: Very — I wouldn't let them go off and write just anything. What if there are ten similar projects already in development? Then everyone's time has been wasted.

M. Bowen: Not very closely. If they're thinking about writing a spec script, I'll sit down with them, ask to hear their four best ideas, and tell them why I think one particular idea is the best if I have an affinity for one. Then they're off and running on their own. I check in on them, but that's about it. When they deliver the script, I may give them a set of notes, but my notes are not very extensive because I don't really look at notes as an agent's place. I have yet to find success micromanaging that process. I'm not an editor, I'm an agent.

M. Blumenthal: Some writers want their agents to work closely with them on their material, others don't. For those clients who want the input I do work closely with them on their material. That may be less common at a large agency. At my company it's part of the service we offer that makes us a strong alternative to the bigger agencies.

W. Niad: We read and give notes on every single script and idea that our writers bring to us. We need to do everything we can to minimize the chance of an exec wanting to pass. Since that's a big part their job — passing — we have to do whatever we can not to give them a single reason to do so.

A. Kolbrenner: I work very closely with my writers; that's what a manager does. Want to write a great script? Rewrite it.

....

Do you have your writers pitch you their ideas first before they write a script?

A. Kolbrenner: Yes, always. Why develop a script on your own only to find out that there is a script exactly like it already in the marketplace?

W. Niad: Yes! If a writer is even thinking about writing a spec, he or she would be stupid not to run the idea past me. That's what I'm here for. A spec is a piece of work that is written with no one paying you to do it, with the hopes that someone buys it when it's finished. This usually takes a good three to four months and sometimes more out of your life, working tirelessly, pouring your heart and soul into it, for the *slight* chance that it may sell. Why wouldn't you want to know if your idea is something that, right now, in this marketplace, is saleable?

All too often, someone gives me a spec and I have to tell them that it's not saleable or that there's another project just like it already being made at a studio. You know you've just crushed the writer and you can practically see him or her deflating right in front of your eyes. It's just heartbreaking.

D. Engel: Writing a spec is such a huge commitment on the part of a writer, both in terms of time and energy, I think it's a good idea for a writer to share his idea with people he trusts before he sets sail.

P. Miller: It depends on the writer. We would never tell a writer what to write, but some writers want our opinion before they go forward.

M. Blumenthal: I encourage writers to pitch their ideas first, before they write a script. Pitching can be useful — for example, to help the writer determine how many other scripts may be out there that are similar. Say you wanted to write *Amistad* but learned that Spielberg was already making it, that might encourage you to come up with another idea.

*Do you expect clients to submit spec scripts for you to sell or do
you look for assignments for them?*

P. Quinn: I expect clients to give me spec material as well as my looking
for assignments for them. If a client does not have a recent successful
produced feature, a terrific spec sale can garner attention and open up
the assignment market. The feature film assignment market is exclusive
and competitive, and studios are attracted to A+ produced writers if they
need to nail a rewrite. I like nothing better than getting a great spec
script from a client, because it can open doors for them for a long time!

A. Kolbrenner: That depends on where they are in their careers. I have
some writers who don't need to write specs any longer, and I have others who need to continue to prove they can write bigger movies.

M. Blumenthal: I do look for assignments for writer clients, that's part of
my job. I also expect clients to submit spec scripts, articles, and pitches
for me to sell — and to help me sell them.

D. Engel: Those two things are not mutually exclusive. They should be
done by both parties concurrently.

P. Miller: Primarily, we deal with spec scripts or adaptations of books that
we already represent.

W. Niad: It really depends on the profile of the client and how that client is
viewed in the industry. An unknown — or relatively unknown — writer
needs to continually generate material. When the writer has garnered
enough fans of their "sample work," only then can they really be considered for assignments. The same is true for a cold client who might at one
point have been the "flavor of the month" and now has fallen to the bottom of the studios' writers lists — if not off the list completely. If they
can't produce a new piece of material to stay competitive with the other
"flavors of the month," their chance of getting work again gets slimmer
and you'll hear, "What have they done lately?" more and more often.

....

Do you send a spec to a few places first to test the waters or does it go wide right away?

W. Niad: In this day and age of computers, testing the waters is nearly impossible. Once a single development exec gets wind of a spec, the title, author, logline, and in many cases even coverage, are all immediately posted on the tracking boards. The mystery and excitement are gone! The ideal process would be giving the script to everyone at the same exact time.

P. Miller: It's best to test the waters by sending it to a few trusted producers with whom you have relationships, and/or talent who may want to attach themselves to it. Many times, it depends on how much confidence you have in a script, and if you are awaiting some feedback before going wide with it.

J. Huddle: No. The only reason to send it out early is if you're trying to get an attachment.

P. Quinn: If I want to get a protected market reaction to a spec, I send it to a few trusted producers and ask them not to get it covered or circulate it — I ask them just to give me their honest opinion of the material. I'm secretly hoping they fall in love it and want to take it in to their studio, but I am also grateful if they just give me a candid read.

M. Bowen: No, because I only go out very selectively with material. At larger agencies, being in the speculative business is not our normal modus operandi. It's a strategy we use to help a client's career along. Smaller agencies eat, drink, and breathe selling spec scripts because that's the way their business is generated. We don't do it that way. When I go out with a piece of material, generally I'm just hoping I can get as many people as possible to read this interesting writer I've just found. I'm not necessarily concerned so much about selling it as I am about introducing the writer to the town. The only time you might take it a little slower is if it is a specialized piece of material and you want to platform it.

M. Blumenthal: Usually a spec script dictates the process by which it's sold. If it's brilliant but on the smaller scale story-wise, we'll send it to actors, directors, and/or smaller financiers to build awareness and interest. If it's a great big concept and terrifically written, we might take it directly to all the studios, or even to producers and studios simultaneously.

A. Kolbrenner: I only send a script out when I know it's ready, then I'll give it to either fans or friends to get some feedback. I'll also throw it into a swimming pool; if it floats, I know it's ready.

....

Is it essential to attach talent to a property before presenting the property for sale? How do you decide?

A. Kolbrenner: Only when that piece of talent helps sell something. If you bring say, a Steve Guttenberg to the table, then not many places will be interested in the property. The decision is also based on the strength of the material, because it may be good enough that talent should come when the movie is set up.

M. Bowen: Absolutely not. It depends on what your agenda is. Talent can help you sell something, — and sometimes it can often help you sell it for a lot — but it may not necessarily be in the best interest of getting that particular project made, or getting that particular client the control he may want in the process. If it's a broad comedy, it's great to have a piece of talent attached because it helps visualize the project, and that can help sell it. But keep in mind that if the person you attached to the project is the hottest guy in town and he's lining up movies left and right, then your client may never see that movie get made — because the studio isn't going to piss off the hottest guy in town to say, "Hey, can you move off this project because you're not available...and let us put someone else on?" So all these situations have to be weighed when moving forward. But if you're a newer writer and you can get a big piece of talent, that's great, hitch your wagon to a star, not a bad way to go. If you're an established writer, your concerns aren't so much about getting a million dollars because you're already there, but rather they're about your control in the process and making sure your movie gets made. Because

I assure you — once you've become an established writer and you're making a lot of money, and you've written say ten specs and all of them have been bought and you've been paid to do rewrites, yet nothing has gotten made — your frustration isn't about how much money is coming in, it's rather, "I went to Hollywood to be a writer for film, not a writer for pleasure."

W. Niad: It is essential to attach elements to anything that is not blatantly commercial, anything that can't sell as a spec. The bottom line is that you have to make a project attractive to a financier, studio, distributor, etc. If it's not a commercial idea, then you need to have other elements that will get people into the theaters.

P. Miller: It isn't essential, as the writing should usually stand alone. However, the current Hollywood climate is very star-driven and an attached star can almost guarantee a studio deal. Usually, if the writing is good enough, Hollywood talent will be drawn to it eventually and subsequently be attached.

M. Blumenthal: Attaching talent to a property before presenting the property for sale is highly valued by the buyers, especially the studio buyers. It's close to being an essential component of getting a big sale these days. But if the property isn't attractive in and of itself, then talent alone won't make a studio want to buy it. There might also be other factors — like budget — which can keep the project from selling. Recently, a very good but not high-concept script went around with a huge star attached. It also had a good, though relatively new, hip young director attached. It's still being considered — but it has not sold.

J. Huddle: It's not essential, but you should always try to attach someone.

....

What is the process of selling a spec script?

M. Blumenthal: The process of selling a spec script involves creating advance awareness of an upcoming project among the buyers, finding the right producer — and/or actor, or director — and leveraging the interested parties to the point of closing a great deal with the right buyer.

Sometimes it happens very quickly, often the process can take weeks. It's a game of keeping people interested. Since so much information about scripts is now available on the Internet, it's hard to control and build on reactions to a piece of material once it's gone into the marketplace.

A. Kolbrenner: Write a great movie that every studio will want to make, get rid of the red flags that make it easy for people to say no, and get it into the hands of the right people who understand what the script is about.

W. Niad: Every studio has a certain number of producer deals. Our job is to first know what type of material each producer is looking for, and second to know which producer at each studio has the greatest chance of having their studio buy something for them. So, in an ideal world, we would pick the best producer for the type of material we're going out with and give them twenty-four hours to pass or bring it in to the studio exec who would then, again in the best of all worlds, read the material in twenty-four hours and decide whether to pass or make a bid.

M. Bowen: Selling a spec script is not a science, but more an art form. It skews more towards high stakes poker than it does high-end math. There are similarities, but it's a different process. First and foremost, you've got to make sure that you get the material out there, then you've got to make sure that you identify the right buyers and producers for that piece of material. What I do is I create a list that has every studio, every independent, every wealthy Wall Street guy who may want to put $20 million into the film business, every buyer in town — then I start to narrow it down to figure out what the logical progression from producer to studio to buyer would be. And then you pick a time and organize your office so you can handle volume in a short period of time. Once you've actually put it out there, you hope that you've set the table well enough, and that the material is strong enough you that a number of buyers are interested. Again, it's not a science, it's more of a feel. It becomes a situation of how to manage the balance between doing what's best for the material, making the most money for the client possible, and not creating a ton of enemies along the way. And that — in the agency world — is the most difficult thing to do, that ultimate balance.

Spec Sells!

One of the most successful spec sales I've been involved with happened to be over a novel. It started in New York with the publishers. They were very high on the book but weren't buying because the author's previous novel had not been a bestseller. Still, the excitement in New York spilled over to the film community in Los Angeles. It had all the studios talking about the novel. But once the studios actually read the book they got cold feet. They all passed. From our perspective there was only one thing left to try — to give it to one of a handful of producers who are powerful enough to turn a "no" into a "yes." If he liked it, it was very likely his studio would buy it for him, despite the fact they had already read it and passed. So we sent the book to this producer, he loved it, got his studio to make an offer. This got the other studios back in the game and, ultimately, also the publishers in New York who had previously passed. The book sold to a great publishing house, became a bestseller, and the movie was made about eighteen months later. It went on to make hundreds of millions at the box office.

—*Marti Blumenthal*

J. Huddle: I can't give you all my secrets, but it's a combination of a good piece of material, a good idea, casting potential, and some degree of salesmanship.

How do you get your client an open writing assignment, and how do you decide which of your clients is best for the job?

A. Kolbrenner: A representative has to be realistic about the clients they represent. If I have a client who has only written small character dramas, I know it's virtually impossible to get him a rewrite of the *Looney Tunes* movie at Warner Bros. Just doesn't work. Knowing your clients and knowing what they are capable of makes all assignments easier. It also saves that executive the time spent reading someone completely inappropriate.

W. Niad: It's fairly simple to decide which client is best for which writing gig. Writers who are hired for assignments are hired after reading samples of the writer's work that shows off elements of what the studio or producer is looking for in a project. The tone should be similar, the character development, the plot, etc. In other words, you wouldn't put a thriller writer up for a Jim Carrey broad comedy, and you wouldn't ask Stephen King to write *Something About Mary*.

When I hear about an assignment that *is* right for a client, the first thing I do is discuss with his or her agent which one of us has the best relationship with each of the executives and producers on the project. Sometimes we all do and so we may all call. That's the beauty of having an agent and a manager. Two or three calls to the exec or producer are sometimes better than one. Between the agent and myself, there's really never an instance where we don't know someone on the project in a decision-making position.

M. Bowen: We put everybody up for a job who seems right for it. That's the broadest of answers. We don't prioritize or discriminate or anything like that. Oftentimes studios have a fairly good idea of who they want based on prior performance. There may be more demand for certain clients than for others. Where it becomes a more interesting scenario is if the studio doesn't see that a particular client might be right for an assignment and you as an agent do. How do you get that client the job? A lot of times the studio tells you who they want and then you have to tell them that the writer they want isn't available. It's the classic bait and switch. They want somebody who's not available and you know someone else who is a very similar type of writer, so you try to suggest him. If the studio people aren't familiar with the new writer, you try to persuade them, you send them the material and you follow up. There's no magic in it, it's a process.

M. Blumenthal: How we decide who the right client for a particular job is and how we get that client that job can be as varied as the clients we represent. We most often work from "inside out," focusing on our clients' strengths to find the right assignment to showcase those strengths in the biggest possible forum...rather than from "outside in," hearing of a job and trying to match the job to the client. We do get those "outside" calls and of course we make sure to suggest the best client for the job, but we find that it is often very productive to work the other way, too.

In deciding who's right for a particular job, the studios look for a writer whose work is most like the job at hand. You probably won't find an executive with the time or incentive to learn about a comedy writer who just happens to know everything about Chinese Triads and really could write a great drama set in that world.

P. Miller: Call the executive and plead with them that our client is the best for the job.

....

How do you manage a large roster of talented clients and give each one the proper attention and effort in developing and maintaining their careers?

M. Bowen: At the United Talent Agency, we fundamentally believe in teamwork as the cornerstone of our business. We wouldn't be able to represent the clients we do and they wouldn't be able to have careers as varied as many of ours do — both in features and television, and as writers, directors, and actors, sometimes all at the same time — if we didn't have people who had different responsibilities for each client. You can't do it alone. That's how you represent a lot of people.

N. Rainford: You don't. There's no way Joe Scribe with a hit series on the air and a greenlit star-driven feature film is going to get the same "attention and effort" as Jack Writer with a three-year-old spec *Friends*. Both may be equally talented, but only one is bringing in the big bonus checks and keeping the agency lights on. My advice...don't ask this question. The fact is, if you're the one with the hit series and greenlit picture you want more than just maintenance from your reps — you want the full court press "top client" servicing. You want your calls answered, meetings set, hefty compensation, access and exposure, and any agent worth their salt knows if they don't deliver, some other agent will. When the studio doors open and all eyes and ears are on you, you won't be thinking about the careers of your agency's other clients, either. Even if you're not yet That Guy, stop keeping score and focus on the goal. *Great writing* is what will make you a better writer and a better client. You've got to keep moving forward and keep moving your team forward. The responsibility is always yours. Don't aim for a "maintained" career. Spend your time writing, creating, and giving your agent the tools he or she needs to sell you more effectively and more enthusiastically. Do the work.

J. Huddle: By having a select group of talented clients about whom I'm very passionate.

P. Miller: You have to maintain a balance between having enough clients to support the business and being able to provide personal attention. Not every client has an active project at all times, so constant contact with every single client is unnecessary.

W. Niad: With a lot of help! There is no way I could manage everything on my own. However, it makes it much easier when you only have clients you love, like I do. It makes working for them fun and makes me even more passionate when I talk about them. Having my own company allows me the ability to carefully choose my clients. Each one is very different from each other, which makes it easy when pitching them. The town knows that if I call to pitch someone, it's going to be one really good, quality writer as opposed to a laundry list of "just okay" writers.

M. Blumenthal: Managing a large roster of talented clients and giving each one the proper attention and effort in developing and maintaining their careers isn't possible. My company works with a select group of high quality artists and works hard to keep the list manageable.

A. Kolbrenner: If you stay close to your clients, you're going know exactly what they are doing at all times and why. Of course, I also drink lots of coffee so I can stay up twenty-four hours a day.

....

How do you work with an agent, manager, and/or attorney?

W. Niad: In an ideal world, we are a united front for the writer. We strategize on what steps to take to get the writer to the next level. On writing assignments, we coordinate which one of us — if not both or all — should call which producer or studio executive. When hyping spec material, two or three voices are always better than one.

D. Engel: It all becomes a big team in mutual support of an artist. If the matches are right, each party will find their strengths in the relationship.

M. Blumenthal: The way I work with a manager or lawyer is the team approach. The chance to work with other experts — to get and use the most information available, to find or close the right deal — is invaluable.

A. Kolbrenner: I work very closely with agents and attorneys. Putting together the right team is crucial to the process. I rarely ask a writer to move from his agent or attorney; it's a decision they should only have to make once. But if a part of the team doesn't work out, it becomes obvious and we move on.

M. Bowen: I think it all depends on the manager. In today's environment, having somebody help an agent triangulate on a situation, to be an extra set of eyes and ears looking at things from a different vantage point, can be very beneficial. However, they aren't always added value. They are sometimes, but not always.

The perfect representation; or how to build a better agent

I have a push-pull theory on representation. Ultimately you want the reps who have push *and* pull, and most importantly, are willing and able to use it on your behalf. The agent would have to personally read and be able to discuss and contribute constructive criticism on all my submitted work. I would take into consideration the other clients the agent represents so as to discern his or her taste in talent. I would need a smart, out-of-the-box thinker, with keen negotiating and selling skills. Professional and personal integrity are a must. No creepy, schmoozy, liar types. But I'd also want someone I liked, someone I could stand being stuck in an elevator with for five hours. That should narrow it down.

—*Nancy Rainford*

What is the current climate between agencies and management companies?

A. Kolbrenner: If you do for them, they do for you. Always has been like that, always will be. We have found success with every agency; however, there are some places that are clearly far and away superior and look to help grow my business as theirs grows as well. Plus, having a client an agency wants to bring over is very important in all the give and take of show business.

M. Blumenthal: The current climate between agencies and management companies is mostly one of accepting each other's existence and working together as productively as possible. Maintaining productive relationships depends on perceiving the various personalities and power bases at each company and understanding the agendas dictated by those factors.

N. Rainford: The lines have been blurred in the past few years. Managers have a stronger presence now than ever before, partly due to the growing number of agents opting into management. Management is less restricted, virtually unregulated, and instantly attainable. Call yourself a manager and you *are* a manager. More importantly you can be a manager and still be a hairdresser, producer, or pro athlete if you so choose. Agents can only be agents. Yes, managers and agents can and do work hand-in-hand, but behind closed doors they still curse one another.

....

How do attorneys fit into the mix?

N. Rainford: In the world of agents and managers there's always room for attorneys. If you land an attorney with great clients, that attorney might use their contacts to get you meetings with agents and managers — but don't expect your lawyer to pitch your spec script to his or her A-list director client. It's not what attorneys do. Even if you've got a power agent, I would still hire an attorney to oversee negotiations and contracts.

A. Kolbrenner: Attorneys can be very helpful in bridging any gaps in the dealmaking process, but I try not to rely on them, or anyone else, for making things happen.

M. Blumenthal: Attorneys come into play mostly at the deal stage. Some attorneys act almost like agents on behalf of their clients — they help sell scripts by giving them to talent or by helping create "the buzz", or advise them on career strategy — but that's more the exception than the rule at the moment.

....

Have you ever had clients taken from you by other agents or managers? Have you done the same?

M. Bowen: What do you think?

W. Niad: Of course. That's the nature of the business. Here I can only speak for myself, but as a manager you devote so much personal time and energy into developing your clients that when they leave, it just crushes you. It feels so personal, like they stabbed you in the back. You try to tell yourself it's just business. If you really can't handle the emotional roller coaster of it all, then you either get out of the business or you become a hardened, embittered, impersonal agent or manager. There are many out there who do choose to operate that way and I often wonder if that may not be the better way. I don't aggressively go after a potential client unless I know or have been told that they are looking to make a move. I think most managers are like that as well as a lot of agents. Stealing clients is really old CAA/Ovitz mentality. I'd like to think things have gotten "nicer." Probably not, though.

P. Miller: Yes, larger agencies have poached us, but I never take another manager's or agent's client. It's just not my style.

A. Kolbrenner: Not yet. I only take on clients who are as excited about working with me as I am about working with them. Most of my clients have become close friends and I plan on representing them for ten or twenty years, until they quit, I quit, or one of us is shoveling shit on a farm. I never try to steal a client — what's the point? If a client is unhappy, he'll come looking for you; going after someone else's clients is a waste of time when you have clients on your roster who need that energy. Spending even ten minutes obsessing about someone else's client seems to be about as ignorant as some managers are.

N. Rainford: Who hasn't? And I'm here to tell you sometimes it really stings. But let's be clear, no one puts a gun to your head and takes you away from your agent. You call the shots and you will all leave your agents. I know, I know — I can name those four who haven't, too — but they are the exceptions that prove the rule. For the smaller agency, holding on to clients once they get some heat is nearly impossible. It's hard to compete with sushi at Matsuhitsu, floor seats for the Lakers, and big agency clout. As far as the clients I've *taken* from other agencies, I like to think they made the switch because I was the better choice, not because I wined and dined them.

M. Blumenthal: Poaching by other agencies is a reality of the business.

J. Huddle: To quote *The Godfather*, "It's the business we've chosen."

....

What is the biggest mistake writers make in their dealings with you?

M. Bowen: They piss me off. They call me bad names. They don't give me gifts at Christmas. That sort of shit really pisses me off.

P. Miller: The biggest mistake is not trusting us to do our jobs and keep them well-informed as to the progress of their project.

W. Niad: Not allowing me to do my job. For example: Sometimes a writer will turn in a script, saying, "I wrote it for this actor and this director and that's who I want you to give it to." It's *my* job to know what the bankable people are looking for. If I know it's not something they would like, I'm not going to send it to them. I take great pride in my reputation for not wasting people's time. Development executives have an inordinate number of scripts to read already; they become resentful if they have to read something we both know they'll never buy...and rightly so! I will not risk my reputation for a writer who just instructs me to do something. My job is to advise and counsel. If you don't want my advice or counsel, then don't hire me.

A. Kolbrenner: Sending material out on their own, or making career decisions without me. Trust is what this is about, its a partnership.

M. Blumenthal: The biggest mistake writers make in their dealings with me usually comes from those who would like to be clients. When they try to convince me that I'm wrong in my belief that I'm not the right person to sell their work they're making a big mistake.

M. Bowen: There are not a lot of things that set me off, because every client is different. I've got clients who scream, clients who cry, clients who are acerbic. There are all sorts of clients, and you just have to be able to handle each one differently. I may get angry because we have a disagreement, but that is part of every relationship, as long as you respect each other's opinions and have a free-flowing communication.

N. Rainford: Years ago television writer and showrunner Karl Schaefer created a subsidized writer's co-op in Hollywood called The 4th Floor. With a sort of think tank philosophy, writers rented office space at a reduced rate and enjoyed the benefits of one another's skills and contacts. Pool tables, vending machines, copiers — all the tools and writer's block breakers were easily accessible. On his door he posted a sign that read SHUT UP AND WRITE.

A Writers' Call To Arms

I think, by and large, that writers are the most underappreciated commodity in the movie business — and I think a large responsibility for that lies in the hands of the writers themselves. If you look at television, if you look at theater, if you look at novels — writers are king. In Hollywood, for whatever reason, writers take a backseat to just about everybody else. That's why I think they need to take a close look at themselves, at how they sell and control their own work. As important as it is for their union to negotiate with the studios for the best financial deals possible, they also need to create a process in which to empower themselves, and not be so willing to play victim to an inequitable system put in place by others. Only then will they find themselves in a better bargaining position for the future. They should be the ones getting the gross, the ones making casting decisions, the ones picking the director — rather than people who don't have the same connection with the material the writer does. So I challenge the writers who are at the very top of their game to consider this and figure out what *exactly* they want to accomplish in the moviemaking process — and to stop being victims.

—*Marty Bowen*

Now to answer your question, new writers have a tendency to submit their material before it's ready for public consumption. Use your SpellCheck, have five other people you trust read your script before you put it out professionally. Listen to constructive criticism. Rewrite, rewrite, rewrite. And as a general rule don't make the mistake of assigning your career to others and neglecting it yourself. I am motivated by my client's motivation. Agent your agent, and, in the words of Karl Schaefer — SHUT UP AND WRITE!

J. Huddle: As you know, writers don't make mistakes.

ATTORNEYS

When do I need an entertainment attorney? Why?

JONATHAN HANDEL: Ideally, you should have an attorney before you sign any agreement. Without an attorney, your dream screenplay may end up on somebody's shelf, unmade, and with little or no compensation for you. Or, you may end up signing an agreement locking you in with a less-than-energetic agent or manager. Without an attorney, and an upfront agreement between you and your writing partner, the day your collaboration breaks down may be the day that the rights to your screenplays become frozen and unsellable.

Of course, in the real world — a term used loosely in Hollywood — you have to balance the risks against the costs. If you can find an attorney to work for you on a percentage basis, then you won't have to pay the lawyer unless you get paid. But, often, you have to pay the lawyer with hard cash, so you need to consider the benefits carefully. There is no easy answer, because you may have to balance a present expense against future risks that may be significant, but might never materialize.

. . . .

If I have an agent or manager, do I need an attorney?

J. Handel: Probably yes. An agent's job is to sell your script and find you work. Most agents don't understand all the ins and outs of a contract, though. They may understand the major deal points, but not the details of the contract itself. That's the lawyer's job. Also, the agent will sometimes consult with the lawyer on deal points or negotiating strategy. A manager's job is to guide your career, whatever that means. Usually it means finding you work, too, although they're not supposed to — in California and New York it's illegal for a manager to procure employment for you. So for any contract, an attorney is essential. Only an attorney can get the details right — and, hopefully, insure that no hidden zingers remain in the contract.

When you get an agent or manager, they'll often — but not always — want you to sign a contract with them, too. Try to get an agent who is "franchised" by the Writers Guild of America — check their Web sites for a list, www.wga.org and www.wgae.org. This gives you at least some assurance that the contract will be reasonable and the agent reputable. Also, agents must be licensed by California and New York state agencies. Unfortunately, managers do not need a license.

You should consider having a lawyer negotiate your agreement with your agent since there are a few negotiable details. For the agreement with your manager, having a lawyer is a must. Too many managers hook their clients with two-year agreements or longer, then lose interest and do nothing after the first few months. Sometimes, the manager will agree to terminate the contract if you ask him. But if not, the contract can be hard to break, or you may be stuck paying a commission to someone who was no help at all.

But no piece of paper is going to completely protect you unless you can afford to sue to enforce it. Developing your intuition about agents and managers isn't easy. You might want to check out a book such as Nancy Rainford's *How To Agent Your Agent* for pointers before you sign any contract.

· ·

Will an attorney "shop" my script?

J. Handel: Some attorneys will try to find buyers for your script. Most won't. That's really an agent's job.

Do attorneys work on commission?

J. Handel: Often, yes, especially if the attorney believes in you, which he probably will if you have an agent and maybe even if you don't. The customary percentage is 5 percent, or occasionally 7½ percent. If you don't have an agent or manager, then 10-15 percent is common.

Other attorneys work on an hourly fee, which can range from $150 for a junior attorney to $400 and above for a maestro. These are LA rates — your mileage may vary. There can also be expenses, which attorneys call "costs." These shouldn't be large though, and will include faxes, long distance phone calls, messengers, copying, and such. Ask in advance, there should be no fancy lunches at L'Restaurant Tres Cher — that's French for expensive, more or less. Lawyers usually need only a PC, phone and fax, not the soup of the day.

Your attorney may also ask for an upfront retainer, which could range from $500 to $2,500, depending on the hourly rate and the complexity of the deal. This is not a monthly fee though, as in "I've got a lawyer on retainer" — those kinds of retainers disappeared the day *Perry Mason* went off the air. Fees and costs are deducted from the retainer and at the end of the deal the remainder of the retainer, if any, is refunded.

Every now and then, very junior attorneys will agree to a flat fee, perhaps $1,500 to $2,500, for a very small and simple deal. They usually regret it, because the deal turns out to be complicated, or the script gets bought and you make a lot of money while the attorney can't make the rent on her cold-water flat. Not that a struggling writer would know what that feels like.

Can I negotiate a deal without a lawyer?

J. Handel: It's a free country, but you get what you pay for. It's well worth paying 5 percent to the lawyer to get a deal done right. But if you can't find a lawyer willing to work for you on commission, or for a price you can afford, you have a few alternatives:

You could ask your cousin — who's a tax lawyer in Kalamazoo — to take a look at the contract. But unless your script's about the IRS, this may cause more harm than good. Entertainment contracts contain provisions that may strike your cousin as curious, or even outrageous. However, many of these are completely customary and non-negotiable. Meanwhile, your cousin is unlikely to know the details of important deal points, or which deal points are missing altogether.

Sometimes your agent will have an attorney who will look over a contract and hit the highlights. Unfortunately, smaller agencies seldom have a lawyer on staff. At larger agencies, your contract probably won't be a priority for the lawyer unless the dollar amounts are large — in which case you'll be able to afford to hire your own attorney anyway.

There are some organizations, such as California Lawyers for the Arts (www.calawyersforthearts.org), that provide consultation for nominal or affordable fees.

Finally, it's very helpful to read books on the business and legal aspects of the entertainment industry, such as Ron Suppa's *This Business of Screenwriting: How to Protect Yourself as a Screenwriter.* Even without an attorney, this will help you understand some of the issues and deal points.

. . . .

If a producer wants my script, and I have an attorney, what's the next step?

J. Handel: The producer offers an option and proposes deal terms, including the dollar amounts. He makes the offer to your agent, if you have one, or to your attorney. The producer and your representative — the agent or attorney — then negotiate the main deal points by phone and perhaps email. If the deal is complex or unusual, the negotiations may involve preparing a deal memo, then revising it back and forth until both parties agree.

Your representative should consult with you during this process and make sure you understand what is being offered, and what counteroffers can or should be made. Ultimately, you must decide whether to take the deal or not.

Once the terms are agreed, the producer prepares a deal memo or a contract. The general rule in all types of movie deals is that the person paying the money drafts the contract. Your lawyer will analyze the deal memo or contract. He then asks the producer to make modifications if the document doesn't match what was agreed to, or if there are details that are too one-sided, both of which are usually the case. If you don't have a lawyer, your agent will review the main deal points, but won't analyze the details. This is where having a lawyer is important.

••

What is an option?

J. Handel: Imagine you finally meet Mr. or Ms. Right. Good-looking, exotic, loves to dance, surf, etc. Um, no, sorry, we're talking business here. I meant imagine you meet a producer who loves your script. Now, this is an industry in which "maybe" means "no," "yes" means "maybe," and "love ya" means nothing at all. But let's assume the producer does want your script. He — she — is willing to pay you major coin — but only if a studio will bankroll the movie and the script purchase. The studio's interested, but won't commit until the producer finds a director and stars. Meanwhile, once one studio likes your script, everyone in town knows about it and they all want it. That's good for you, but maybe not for the producer. Remember, he still doesn't own the script, yet he's got to find a director and stars. All those meetings at the Polo Lounge, all those days chatting up hot young actors poolside at the Beverly Hills Hotel, those expensive dinners at Spago, and, well, yes, the twelve-hour days spent making literally hundreds of calls, sending out dozens of scripts, and hearing "no, not interested" every hour on the hour. Yes, producing is hard work. And for what? Since the producer doesn't own the script, suppose he does find a director and stars. Another producer could swoop in at the last moment and offer you twice as much as the first producer was going to pay, knowing that the elements (director and stars) are already attached.

So, before doing all the work, maybe the producer should first nail down your script by paying you major coin upfront, but that's a big financial risk unless a studio is interested — and now we're back to square one. See the problem? What we have here is a failure to commit. The solution: an option, which is a contract between you and the producer that allows him to control the script without buying it outright. The contract says that for some time period — one year, for instance, or eighteen months — no one else can buy the script. If you want to sell it during that time, you can only sell to the producer. In fact, if the producer wants to buy, you *must* sell it to him, unless the option period has expired. The option specifies the price as well. No negotiating later — the negotiation is all up front. If the producer exercises the option, he sends you a notice and payment, and the script is his.

Why would you do this — why let someone control your master-piece without buying it? Three reasons: One, because you usually have no choice — no producer is going to pay you hard cash unless he knows there's a studio willing to pay him. Two, because the producer's going to do the hard work of attaching a director and stars, and selling the screenplay to a studio. And, three, because the producer pays you for the option itself, as well as for the script if he later buys it. The accepted standard for option price is 10 percent of the agreed purchase price of the script itself. If the producer later buys the script, the option payment is generally applied against the purchase price. The option agreement usually also gives the producer the right to have you do two or three revisions, for a specified price. And, the option may be extendable, again for an additional payment, which is usually not applicable against the purchase price. There are a lot of other important details, which is why you may want to have an attorney.

....

Should I offer a free option on my screenplay?

J. Handel: If you're a new writer, just finding a producer seems like a great thing, and often it is. However, the producer may not want to pay you for the option, since he's taking a risk on a newcomer. This is disappointing, but common. Before you agree, make sure the producer will work hard and knows the right people in the business. If you can help it, don't agree to an option longer than one year. You can try to negotiate a shorter period, but most producers will tell you that it's hard to do anything in less than a year. And they're right.

....

What's the difference between an "option agreement" and a "writer agreement" or "writing services agreement"?

J. Handel: An option agreement relates to the purchase of material you've already written — a spec script, which means one that you wrote in the speculative hope that you'd be able to sell it. A writing services agreement, also called a writer agreement, is an agreement for you to write a script for a producer at his or her request, for a fee. As noted above, an option agreement usually also includes the provisions of a writing services agreement, so that the producer can have you prepare revisions to your script if he so desires.

What if I'm a writer-director?

J. Handel: You would also have a directing services agreement. If you're only going to sell the script if you can direct, then the option agreement needs to say this as well, so that the obligation to hire you as director stays attached to the script. Of course, this will make it much harder to sell the script.

How does a book option work?

J. Handel: If you wrote the book, the producer will want to option all motion picture and television rights, and certain related rights. In contrast, with a screenplay, the producer usually options all rights. He may then hire a screenwriter to write the script.

If someone else wrote a book, and you want to write a screenplay based on it, don't — unless you can buy or option the motion picture and television rights to the book. The producer must to have those rights in order to make a movie. If you write a screenplay based on the book, but don't have the rights, your screenplay will be wasted effort if the rights can't be obtained. Usually, producers won't consider a spec script based on a book if the screenwriter hasn't obtained the rights.

What is a deal memo?

J. Handel: A deal memo is a short contract, typically one or two pages, that spells out the main terms of the deal. A deal memo is legally binding if signed by both parties.

As an example, a deal memo for an option might include:
• Names and addresses of the parties

- Title of the script
- Term (time period) of the option
- Option price (price for the option itself)
- Purchase price (price to buy the script)
- What rights are optioned (for a screenplay, it's usually all rights)
- The term and price of any option extension
- Credit (your name onscreen and in ads)
- The nature and fees for any writing services (revisions) to be performed at the producer's request if the option is exercised
- What payments must be made if there are sequels or TV series based on your story

....

How long is a standard contract?

J. Handel: A motion picture option agreement is typically six to eight pages, plus three pages of exhibits. A writing services agreement might be slightly shorter. On the other hand, if the agreement includes net or gross profits, these may be defined in an attachment to the contract that is several times longer than the contract itself.

....

What's a collaboration agreement?

J. Handel: An agreement between two writing partners that specifies how the work, fees, decision-making, and ownership are divided. What happens if one partner isn't pulling his or her weight, or the partners disagree on whether to do a particular option deal? Who owns the script if the partners break up? The collaboration agreement addresses these questions. You may love each other now, but breakups are frequent, and can be ugly.

....

What's a submission agreement?

J. Handel: An agreement a studio or producer may require you to sign before they will look at your script. The agreement says that you understand that the studio or producer may be working on the exact same type of script as the one you submit, and that you waive most of your legal rights. Most producers will require new or unrepresented writers to sign a submission agreement. The agreement sounds unfair — in fact, it sounds like an invitation for theft — but producers want to protect themselves from unjustified lawsuits.

Can I copyright my script by mailing it to myself?

J. Handel: No. This question confuses two different things — copyright and registration — but the answer is no in any case.

Copyright is federal law that prohibits anyone else from reproducing or distributing your script, or making a movie or TV show based on it — unless you give them the right to do so. An option agreement, when exercised, transfers those rights to the producer — now he has those rights, and you do not.

Under copyright law, your script is copyrighted the moment you type it into the computer. You don't have to put the copyright symbol © on it, and you don't have to send it to the Copyright Office in Washington, DC.

There are some good legal reasons to use the copyright symbol, thus, you may want to put a copyright notice on your cover: Copyright © [year] [your name].

> *Given the fact that ideas are not copyrightable, how does a writer protect a synopsis, which reveals critical and unique elements of one's screenplay, from "theft" once that synopsis is published on the Internet?*
>
> The simple answer is: "You can't." If your work isn't in some copyrightable form, you risk losing it with no recourse. I've been told that legitimate entertainment companies are not in the business of ripping off people's ideas, but that isn't the whole world. Theft of idea cases are very difficult to make and win. First of all, they are based on an implied contract. Second, there's a one-year statute of limitations. And third, the only jurisdiction that recognizes them is California. Since privity of contract — you've disclosed your idea with the expectation of being paid by the person to whom you've disclosed — is required, with whom do you have the implied contract when you post your ideas on the Web? Your best bet is getting something into a form you can copyright and doing the registration before you post.
>
> *—Christine Valada*

However, doing so is not customary in the business, so this is an area where you may have to trade off appearances against some legal protection.

. . . .

Should I register my script?

J. Handel: There also are good reasons to register your script for copyright with the federal Copyright Office (www.copyright.gov). There is a small fee — currently $30 — so you may want to be selective as to which drafts you register. Again, you do not have to register your script in order for it to be protected by copyright.

You may also want to register your script with the Writers Guild. There's an online registry that will let you register your script from a menu in Final Draft, or you can visit www.wga.org. The fee is currently $20. Registration proves that you had a copy of the script as of a certain date. It doesn't prove that you're the author, so there's some disagreement as to whether registration has legal value. As an aside, registering a script with the Writers Guild has nothing to do with being a member of the Writers Guild.

Registration does mean that you can put "reg. WGA [registration number]" on the cover of your script. Unlike copyright notices, this notice is quite customary. Most people in Hollywood think that the notice has legal implications, and that may have the practical effect of deterring theft of your script or idea.

Mailing the script to yourself might seem to be the equivalent of registering it with the Writers Guild. However, envelopes can be steamed open, postmarks are sometimes missing or illegible, and the whole process is just considered unprofessional.

. . . .

Can I trademark my script?

J. Handel: No, probably not. People sometimes say "trademark" when they mean "copyright." Trademark protects logos, names of products and services, and tag lines. The title of scripts, books, and movies can sometimes be trademarked, but only if it is the title of a series, not a single work. For instance, "Planet of the Apes" can be trademarked, because there are several movies and TV series that have that phrase in their titles.

....

Someone stole my script, or my idea — what can I do?

J. Handel: Maybe nothing. Copyright infringement requires "access" and "substantial similarity." In other words, whoever "stole" your work would have to have seen your script and created something similar. How do you know they did? And how similar is the other script? These are questions that need to be answered first. Also, copyright protects the *expression* of ideas, not the ideas themselves (defining the distinction would take an entire book). It's very difficult to protect ideas, and similar ideas are almost always in the air, occurring to multiple people at the same time.

If you really, truly think your work has been infringed, consult a lawyer, preferably one who will take the case on contingency. But first, write a short memo. Explain exactly how and why the other person obtained a copy of your script. Then, include a table that lays out, side by side, each similarity between your script and theirs. Entertainment lawyers hear many, many claims of supposed infringement. Most are probably unfounded. You need to persuade the lawyer that yours is not.

....

What are deferments, net profits, gross profits, and residuals — and how do I get some?

J. Handel: Let's start with what we've already discussed:

Option Payments are the payment of the option purchase price or option extension price.

The Script Fee or Purchase Price is the payment for purchase of the script.

The Writing Services Fee is the fee paid for your writing services — rewriting a script, or writing a script when you've been hired by a producer.

These are sometimes called Fixed Compensation, Basic Compensation, or Guaranteed Compensation to distinguish them from the items listed below, which are sometimes referred to as Contingent Compensation:

A Deferment is a fee paid to you if something happens in the future. For instance, a very low budget picture may involve a deferment and little or no guaranteed compensation. The deferment should get paid if the movie is sold to a distributor. Other deferments may be payable if the film reaches a certain level of box office receipts, or other conditions, but these are usually only for established writers.

Net Profits are theoretically a percentage of the net profits of the film. Writers frequently get five net points, i.e., 5 percent of the net profits. But here's the rub: "Net profit" in the film industry doesn't actually mean "net profit" as used in any other business. Instead, there are multi-page contract provisions that define "net profits" such that they usually amount to zero. For this reason, they are also known as Net Proceeds, Defined Proceeds, or various other terms, mostly unprintable.

Gross Profits refer to a percentage of total monies brought in, or the gross — but like ice cream, gross can come in many flavors: first dollar gross, adjusted gross, gross with reduced fees, rolling breakeven, and mint chocolate chip (if only). They actually do amount to something, sometimes many millions of dollars, which is why they are reserved for top directors, stars, producers, and occasionally top writers.

Residuals are sort of like net profits, except that they do amount to something. They're payments based on the use of a movie in media other than in domestic theaters — for instance, home video, TV, overseas release, etc. Residuals are part of the Writers Guild agreement, so you only get them if you're writing for a company that is a Guild signatory, which generally also means that you are a Guild member.

··

How do I become a member of the Writers Guild?

J. Handel: The short answer is that you do so by selling a script to a company that is a signatory to the Writers Guild Agreement, or by performing writing services for them. Contact the Writers Guild for more information.

Is it possible to retain the rights to your characters — names, appearance, etc. — for other projects once you've sold your screenplay?

DINA APPLETON and DANIEL YANKELEVITS: Unfortunately, it is extremely unlikely that a studio will allow a screenwriter to retain motion picture rights to his characters once the studio acquires the screenplay. In today's universe, where almost every successful film generates a sequel — even *Gladiator*, where the main character was killed off in the initial film — studios expect to acquire *all* rights to the character for spin-offs, toys, video games, etc. However, if a writer retains a skillful negotiator to make his deal, the writer will almost certainly be granted a first opportunity to be engaged to write the sequel film. Thus, if the author wrote *A Giant Hit* for Miramax, Miramax would need to offer the writing gig for *A Giant Hit 2* to that same writer (most likely with a "floor," or minimum price, no less than that paid for the first film). In addition, the Writers Guild will require that certain royalties be paid to the credited writer of the first film when his or her characters are used in spin-offs or other productions. Established authors may be able to extract a few additional rights, such as the right to mount live stage productions based on their work, but these details are worked out on a case-by-case basis.

This answer is a bit different in the case of books. Authors of books almost always retain the right to exploit "author-written sequels" — at least in book form. Accordingly, a writer such as Tom Clancy (author of the Jack Ryan books), can utilize his characters in new stories and sell the print publication rights to those stories without the movie studio's involvement. However, Paramount — the studio that released the first Jack Ryan film — almost certainly retained a right of first negotiation, as well as a "matching" right of *last* refusal, to acquire the motion picture rights for subsequent Jack Ryan books. Thus, when Clancy finishes a new Jack Ryan book, he must negotiate with Paramount before shopping the book to other studios. Moreover, if he does not make a deal with Paramount, he cannot sell it to a third party, such as Disney, without offering Paramount the opportunity to match Disney's last offer. This makes it extremely unlikely that Disney will usurp Paramount's successful franchise.

What if I sold an option to a script that now appears to be going nowhere with the company that bought it, but there is another producer who might be interested? Is there any way of getting the first buyer to release his rights without having to pay back the entire option fee?

LARRY ZERNER: There are several possibilities, but the first one is to *just ask*. If the script isn't going anywhere with this company, they may just be willing to give you back the rights, figuring that if they can't sell your script, there's no way you're going to be able to do so. If they won't just give you the rights back, then the next question is, "What will they take instead?" You could offer a pro-rated sum on the option price — i.e., if the option price was $1000 for two years, and there is six months left on the option, offer them $250 for the remaining half year. If you have a serious buyer, that would be a small price to pay. If you really don't have the cash, see if your "interested" producer will advance you the money to get out of the option. If he is really interested in your script and wants to option it himself, the extra money needed to get your script out of the current option should not be a problem.

You might also offer the current option holder a piece of any money you receive in the event that your script is sold during the remainder of the option term. The current option holder is probably worried that if he gives you back the rights to the script, you'll sell it and he'll look like a chump. By giving him a piece of any potential sale, you can alleviate the fear that he's giving away the rights to a potential blockbuster. Also, if you had another script that the option holder might like, you could offer him an option on the new script in exchange for releasing the old one. Since he's had no luck with your first script, he might be willing to exchange it for something new.

Using one or a combination of these ideas should get you your script back, but if not, then you're just going to have to wait until the option runs out. That is why it is important to limit your option periods to as short a period of time as possible, preferably no more than one year, with the opportunity for the option holder to pay for additional extensions. By keeping the option period shorter, you make sure that the producer is not sitting on your script, but is working hard to get it sold. And, by making him pay for extensions, you ensure that the producer doesn't hold onto the rights after his interest has waned.

....

What if I'm writing a script in which a celebrity look-alike will play the real-life person in the film — do I need to get approval from the celebrity or their family before I can use their likeness?

L. Zerner: Using a celebrity look-alike in a movie does not constitute a copyright violation, as nobody can own a copyright on his or her appearance. However, if you were going to have Spiderman or Mickey Mouse appear in your movie, that *could* lead to a copyright infringement lawsuit because the characters themselves are copyrighted. (While there are certain exceptions in the case of parodies, that is a different question than the one we're answering here). The main issue that arises when portraying real people is the possibility of a lawsuit for defamation. If the celebrity is dead, you don't have to worry because the dead cannot be defamed. But let's say that you have a scene where Meryl Streep robs a bank — she could sue you for falsely portraying her as a bank robber.

While you need to make sure that nothing in your script will get you sued, for most writers, I would simply tell them to not worry so much about the legal stuff, and just write the best script they can. If the script is good, the producer will figure out a way to make it work. Look at Charlie Kaufman (*Being John Malkovich, Adaptation*). He writes incredible stuff with celebrities doing amazing things — John Malkovich has a portal into his brain! Susan Orleans is a drug-dealing murderer! — but because his scripts are so creative and original, the producers were able to convince the celebrities to give permission to use them as characters in his movies.

....

If I have the rights to do a screenplay on the life of a real person, do I need to get the rights to other people in their life, like an ex-wife?

L. Zerner: Ideally, when you are writing a screenplay about a real person who is not a public figure, you want to obtain rights from as many of the people who will be portrayed in the screenplay as possible. In fact, if you try to sell your screenplay to a producer and you *haven't* obtained such rights, it may result in the deal falling apart. You also may not be able to obtain insurance if you haven't properly cleared all the rights.

By acquiring these rights, you have obtained an agreement from these people that they will not sue you if the screenplay or motion picture defames them or invades their right of privacy or right of publicity. If you do not obtain these rights in advance, then you run the strong risk that you will be sued once the film is released.

If it is impossible to obtain rights from these people, then you should make changes to the characters so that they are not identifiable as real people. However, it may not be enough just to change the names of the people involved. If the character is still identifiable because of his relationship with the main character (i.e. his boss), then you might need to change the relationship so as to reduce the risk of identification — for example, change the boss to a district supervisor.

If a character such as the ex-wife is crucial to the story, do your utmost to obtain rights from her. Otherwise, you should figure out a way to either minimize her importance in the story or else change her character to that of an old girlfriend.

ASK THE PROS
MENTORS

ASK THE PROS

MENTORS

How do I choose which genre is best for my story?

JOHN TRUBY: The single most important decision you must make when developing your script's premise is: What genre should I use? You may come up with a terrific one-line idea for a movie, but if you don't develop it the right way, the best scene writing in the world won't make a difference.

Genre describes a particular type of story — such as detective, comedy, thriller, or action. The reason genre is so important is because virtually all Hollywood filmmaking is based on it. That sounds like a pretty extreme statement until you look at how Hollywood has set itself apart from the rest of the world. The rest of the world has always emphasized original artistic vision in their filmmaking, which is great for art, but bad for commerce because it forces the audience to re-invent the wheel for each film. They have to guess whether they want to enter the theater. And they have to work hard to figure out the unique story patterns that make that film work.

Hollywood realized a long time ago that it was not in the business of selling original artistic vision (though it sometimes happens anyway). It is in the business of buying and selling story forms. Genres tell the audience up front what to expect from the product they are buying. If they like a particular kind of story, chances are they will like this particular film, especially if the writer and director give the expectations a little twist.

For years, Hollywood films were only one genre at a time — say western, detective, or family comedy. Then someone had the brilliant idea, "Hey, let's give them two for the price of one." That's why virtually every film made now is a combination of two or three genres. The implications for you as a writer in Hollywood are huge. First, you have to figure out what genres are best for your idea. Second, you have to know those genres better than everyone else. Third, you have to know how to transcend the forms so you can give the audience a sense of originality and surprise.

The problem with genre is that each one is a complex system of story, with its own unique hero, opponent, story beats, structures, and themes. Fortunately, this information, though complex, is knowable. You just have to put in the time and effort to learn it. When I first start developing a story, I look at a number of elements to help me choose which genres will get the most out of the idea. The first element is the hero's role in the story. When you look at your premise, you can usually imagine a basic action that the hero would take throughout the story. For example, is the hero essentially a fighter (Action), a lover (Love), an enforcer or criminal (Crime), an endangered investigator (Thriller), or a victim (Horror)?

A second element to look at is your hero's desire line. This represents your hero's particular goal over the course of the story. It provides the spine of the story, so every hero should have one. It just so happens that each of the major genres is associated with a particular desire line. One way to get a sense of the best genre for your idea is to match the probable desire line of your hero to the key desire line of each genre. For example, the desire in a fantasy is to explore an imaginary world. In myth, it's to go on a journey that ultimately leads to one's true self. In sitcoms, the hero wants to escape from an impossible predicament. In thrillers, the hero's desire is to escape attack. In detective stories, the hero wants to find the truth.

An opponent who fights the hero and tries to prevent him or her from reaching their goal is another important element that helps determine your genre. The relationship between hero and opponent is the most important relationship in your story. A good opponent must be a unique individual but also fulfill a crucial story function. For example, in television drama, the main opponents are usually other family members. In comedy, the opponents tend to be various expressions of society at large. In love stories, the main opponent is the lover.

Another way that the various genres set themselves apart from one another is that they each ask a different central question or force the hero to make a crucial decision. The key question in thrillers: Is your suspicion justified? In comedy: Do you lie or show your true self? In action: do you choose freedom or life? In detective stories: Who is guilty and who is innocent? Part of exploring your premise has to do with discovering the particular key question your hero must confront. How your hero answers this question is the real meat of the story. It's what makes the audience want to watch this character all the way to the end. One of the benefits of genre is that a framework for these questions has already been worked out. You just provide the details and the variations. Keep in mind that when you explore your premise, you are at the very beginning of the writing process. So you may not know the key question your story will ask. The important thing is to make a guess now. It will help you extend and focus your idea, as well as lead you to the best genre for carrying the story.

Genres aren't just systems for expressing certain themes either, they are also strategies for storytelling. Action stories set up a kind of heavyweight fight with an intense punch/counterpunch between hero and opponent. Science fiction sends the hero to a unique technological future that highlights strengths and weaknesses in the present world. Thriller places a weakened hero in a tight box and shows him or her struggling to escape. Crime pits a criminal who thinks he is above society against a defender of society's rules and values.

The above elements, though helpful, only tell you which genres are probably best for your idea. They don't tell you how to write them. Writers typically underestimate the difficulty in mastering a genre. Each one is filled with story beats and themes that are highly choreographed. That's why I always recommend that writers give genres intense study and specialize in no more than three. I know a lot of talented writers, but I know no one who has mastered more than three or four genres.

BUZZ WORD
MOW – Abbreviation for movie-of-the-week. Used in entertainment trade papers and on union forms.

One final caution: Don't look down your nose at genre writing. First, because it's a bad business decision — the entire entertainment industry is based upon it — second, because genres can actually make you a better writer. Most writers go their whole lives without finding their voice. Learning which genres are best for you often crystallizes what is uniquely you and lets you write from your strengths. You still have to do each genre story in an original way. But harnessing the power of genre will take you a long way toward your goal of being a top professional writer.

....

How in-depth do I need to go with a character's backstory before I start writing the script?

LINDA COWGILL: You can never go wrong if you know as much as possible about your character. Who she is and what he does, where he comes from, who she loved — all these things contribute to your understanding of the character and therefore your ability to make that character seem real.

I must admit that I don't do lengthy character biographies on my own characters. But the characters who have been the most successful in my own scripts have been the ones I know the best, either because they're the closest to me and those I've known in biographical detail, or because I've spent time getting to know them in the writing process.

The thing is, when you know a character inside and out, it's not about inventing the key detail that makes the character feel true, because the details emerge through his or her thoughts, words, and actions.

Not every story will demand a lot of backstory and therefore the character background to tell it well. Sometimes you just need just a detail or two. In the film *Chinatown*, we don't know where Gittes comes from or who his parents were, but we don't need to know. We know he used to be a cop, and there was a girl once, in Chinatown, and he couldn't save her. In an early draft of the script, Robert Towne gives two pages between Evelyn and Gittes to paint in the details of this past relationship, but later all that detail is cut and just comes down to a few sentences and feelings that do it perfectly.

Ultimately it comes down to feeling that you know enough to start writing. In the writing, you're going to discover more.

··

How do I find the right balance between action and character in my script?

L. Cowgill: When we think of plot, we usually think in terms of action. But action is driven by what the characters want and the conflict that stands in their way. The basic parameters of plot give a story direction and meaning — characters act on their desire, which leads to action, which in turn leads to conflict. But drama is as much about the repercussions of an action as it is about the action itself. It's not just the momentum of action that frames the story, but how characters respond to the action that ultimately conveys meaning to the audience. Is a character devastated when his lover rejects him, or secretly relieved? After arguing with his wife, does the protagonist unload his anger on his daughter and feel bad about it? Does he go get drunk? Does he sit on the porch and feel sorry for himself? Different outcomes lend different interpretations to the material. The audience needs to see the results of action — the consequences, the effect — to fully understand the dramatic weight action carries. The emotional reaction to action, the blowback of desire, is often where the heart of your drama lies.

That is why plotting a story is more than just mapping out specific steps a character takes toward his goal within a conflict. It is structuring action and emotion to achieve an intended effect. We want to make the audience feel a variety of emotions throughout a story — tension, excitement, fear, frustration, joy — and not just at the end. Action carries us along, but emotion adds dimension, ups the stakes, increases empathy or antipathy, and creates meaning.

Orchestrating a character's emotional growth or regression allows the audience to experience the story with him. It helps develop the character's transformational arc more fully by creating an outline or pattern of emotions that evolves in relationship to the action. This pattern can't progress willy-nilly (as it may appear to in life), but must be ordered to make sense logically. When conceived and executed properly, the emotional pattern of the plot, reflected and defined in the protagonist, will deepen the audience's understanding of every factor in the story.

Is it better to always do a treatment first, or, if I have the whole idea and plot in my head, am I better off just going straight into the first draft of the script?

L. Cowgill: Everyone is going to work differently. If you can work out a story in your head and know — or at least have a good idea — of where it's going in the second half, then working out the details in a first draft can be great. I always find writing the actual script more fun that working out an outline. But you have to realize that this first draft is more your outline than a "working" first draft. You're still discovering the details of the story and it will need at least one rewrite, or maybe even a dozen, before it's finished.

The key here is having something as a whole in mind before starting. I now won't go to script unless I've worked out the story fully. For me and my process, that means writing notes and ultimately a synopsis. I don't do scene-by-scene outlines anymore because I still like the process of discovery that happens going from synopsis to script. But when I work with students who are starting from scratch, I absolutely have them do either a beat sheet or an outline to begin. And even when they are doing a rewrite, scene-by-scene outlining saves a lot of time and work in terms of seeing the story as a whole.

If my screenplay is a fictional story, why is it important to research it before writing?

DYANN S. RIVKIN: To succeed, a movie depends on what's known as a "willing suspension of disbelief." For some two hours of time you are asking an audience to believe that the world of your story is real, and to believe that the characters in your story are real. To accomplish this, you must use research make your characters and your story as true to life as they can be.

To create characters who are fully-developed individuals rather than superficial stereotypes, you may need to interview and get to know people similar to your characters — people of the same ethnic group, same age, same occupation, people who participate in the same activities, who travel in the same social spheres. If you only write characters based other characters you've seen in movies or on TV, you run the very real risk of perpetuating stereotypes rather than developing your own unique and three-dimensional characters.

As you research your characters, you'll find that most people love to talk about themselves: their lives, professions, problems, and dreams. When talking to a writer, people generally will want to make sure you understand every detail of their world and their lives. For legal reasons, be sure the people you interview for your research know that you are not directly basing any particular character on them personally, but rather trying to gain a deeper understanding of people like them in order to create believable characters.

Researching your characters is also important because in dialogue, a character's choice of words, sentence structure, and speech patterns will usually reveal something of the character's nature, origins, workplace, and personality. Knowing your character's backstory gives you the opportunity to research the speech patterns and vernacular of the region he or she comes from. If you are able to talk with people from the area where your characters were born and raised, and also from the region where your story is set, this will enrich your dialogue and make your characters more credible.

It is also very important to research the world in which your story is set — the time period, place, culture, customs, social mores, and so on. Doing detailed research on the setting of your story will help you create a world that is real and believable on the screen.

As you research your characters and the setting for your story, you'll likely make discoveries that will spark other ideas you can use in your screenplay. And, by creating full-bodied characters and a world for your story that is true-to-life, you'll be ensuring that your screenplay offers a believable reality for the script reader and the producer who will read it — and ultimately, for the audience who will see your movie and identify with, and become involved in, the characters and the world you have created on the page.

Which path should a writer take — strive for uniqueness or adhere to popular themes?

L. Cowgill: I don't mean to sound glib, but both. Obviously, you want to be noticed. You always want your work to be fresh and unique, but if it's so far off from what your audience will pay for, you're not going to get anyone to put up the money for you to make your film. You have to develop your own voice, but to have a real career, you also need to be sure that your creative voice speaks to others. If you can be unique but still tell a story your audience wants to hear, that's the best of both worlds.

Can you rewrite too much? Is there such a thing as overworking a script?

L. Cowgill: This is a tough question to answer because on one side there's the belief that if you keep working a script it will only get better. And usually that's what happens. Things do get better. But there comes a point when one of two things happens:

On the positive side, you've worked it so far that now you're just tweaking this or that, and really the piece is what it is. No amount of tinkering with it is going to change it. It's time to take it out and see what happens in the real world. Going through and doing another rewrite isn't going to improve its salability: Either people are going to like it as is or they're not.

On the negative side, writers can take a script that has reached a stage where it's pretty strong, or even one that never evolved quite right, and keep working it until they lose it altogether. We see this with writers who aren't completely clear on what they want from their stories, or when they keep trying to please too many people.

This process happens in script development too, where a script that starts out strong gets purchased and taken in for rewrites. Usually there are just too many people involved in the process, so the writer has too many people to please. It's the old "too many cooks spoil the stew" syndrome, and most scripts don't survive the process. Occasionally, someone comes along and gets it right, but that's a happy accident as far as I'm concerned.

....

As I write, I have an image in my mind as to what the scene should look like, but I know camera direction is best left to the director. What guidance, if any, should I provide?

L. Cowgill: How you put your narrative parts of the story together can be very visual if you consider your words carefully. You're right to shy away from camera directions, because nothing irritates readers more than having to read them. But how you describe the action can give a strong indication of how we're seeing the action play. My advice is to tell your story *as you see it*. If you write: "She picks up the bill on the table. It says in bright, bold red: OVERDUE," any director worth his salt is going to know showing the "OVERDUE" is important and will go to a close-up of it. Write what you see, clearly, and in the hands of a good director it will be shot that way.

....

How do I find the right writing partner?

CLAUDIA JOHNSON and MATT STEVENS: Some of the greatest movies and TV series have been written by script partners, from Billy Wilder's legendary collaborations with Charles Brackett and I.A.L. Diamond to the Academy Award-winning work of the Coen Brothers. Each year the list of script partners and their successes grows longer. Why? Because collaborative scriptwriting is one of the most productive and successful ways to write...*if you find the right writing partner*.

"Okay," you may be thinking, "but how do I do that?" It's a question many writers have asked us since we started our collaboration, and a question we've asked many collaborative writers. And while there's no one-size-fits-all answer, there are some strategies that can help, whether you're looking for a partner to co-write a project, or someone with whom to share a writing career.

Collaboration is such an intimate creative relationship, it's best to begin looking for a prospective partner among the people you know. You have a greater chance of working successfully together if you've worked out the bugs of *being* together. So it's no surprise that most of the teams that we talked to evolved out of close personal relationships — friends or family or lovers. "We knew each other so well before we even started, and that's crucial," Andrew Reich says of his collaboration with Ted Cohen, both head writers and executive producers of *Friends*.

Like Reich and Cohen, Scott Alexander and Larry Karaszewski, and Matt Manfredi and Phil Hay (*crazy/beautiful*) met in college and were best friends before they began writing together. Fay and Michael Kanin (*Teacher's Pet*, *The Opposite Sex*), Nicholas Kazan and Robin Swicord (*Matilda*), and Lee and Janet Scott Batchler (*Batman Forever*) chose each other as spouses before they chose each other as writing partners. Olivier Ducastel and Jacques Martineau (*Adventures of Felix, Jeanne and the Perfect Guy*) fell in love before they fell into their collaboration, "It was for us, first and foremost, a relationship as lovers."

Then there's brotherly or sisterly love. That's not to say other familial combinations aren't possible — the father-son team of Sherwood and Lloyd Schwartz springs to mind — but the sibling collaboration is far more prevalent: the Ephron sisters, and the Coen, Wachowski, Farrelly, and Weitz brothers, to name just a few.

But what if you don't have a partner-worthy friend, spouse, lover, or sibling? If you can't find a collaborator among the people you know, get to know more people! As the group of writers you know expands, so do your chances of finding the right writing partner. If you're in college, wake up and smell the collaborations! Enroll in film or screenwriting classes. Or join a drama or comedy group. If you're not in college, *nil desperandum*, take classes anyway. Attend writers' conferences. Join writers' organizations. Socialize. If you *still* can't find a collaborator among contacts and colleagues, consider posting an ad:

Writer-director seeks scriptwriting partner. Goal: Funny movies that are completely original and totally unlike Hollywood's endless parade of remakes. Ideally your forte is solid character development. Please contact me. Are we a match?

Hey, if you can find Mr. or Ms. Right with an ad, why not the right writing partner? You can post notices, as many do, in any number of places on the Internet. You can also place ads in publications such as

Variety, The Hollywood Reporter, Backstage, the *Los Angeles Times, Screenwriter Magazine,* and *Hollywood Scriptwriter* — and their online versions as well.

Whatever venue you choose — finding the perfect partner among people you know or among perfect strangers — it's essential to find someone with the qualities crucial to a good partnership. We have to be honest — we hated each other the first time we met on the faculty of the Florida State University Film School. But as we worked together on students' scripts, we discovered that we had similar sensibilities about what makes a good story. And perhaps more important, we had the same sense of humor. We cracked up at each other's jokes.

Let's face it — it's hard to have contempt for someone who laughs at your jokes. Humor studies show that this is one of the most powerful ways to reverse a bad first impression — which is why Matt laughs a lot on first dates.... Such is the power of humor in creating human connections, and good collaborations. In fact, the same sense of humor between you and your partner may predict, as nothing else can, a closeness and compatibility in your writing life. "Say something that you think is funny, and if the other person doesn't laugh, run — *do not walk* — to the next candidate," says Larry Gelbart (*Caesar's Hour, M*A*S*H*). "The same rule applies to a pair of writers who want to do drama, action, whatever, except without the laughs. What do you like? Who do you like? Which movies? Which this? Which that?"

Equally as important as finding a partner who you are compatible with is knowing their work, and how it might compliment your own. If you haven't already, read something they've written. Request a writing sample and offer one of yours. If you don't like their writing, or vice versa, keep right on moving to the next candidate.

"I think collaborations are much more successful when people have different strengths," says Peter Tolan (*Analyze This, Analyze That*). "The best collaborations are when you shore up each other's weaknesses." It's important to keep this in mind as you search for a partner: "You're looking for someone hopefully with complementary strengths," says *Batman Forever* co-writer Batchler, "but that means that you have to have an understanding of your own strengths."

"I think you have to be remarkably self-aware to say, 'I can do that and that; I just can't do *that,*'" adds Tolan, because in any successful collaboration, partners have to play to their strengths.

Marshall Brickman and Woody Allen (*Annie Hall, Manhattan*) certainly understood their complementary strengths. "I tend to be somewhat more bound by logic than Woody," Brickman explains, "and I say that as a criticism of me rather than of him. His approach to a problem or material in general is more intuitive than mine. I like to kind of back into things logically; he seems to have a genius for making some kind of intuitive leap, which defies logic but solves the problem." This complementary nature gives each collaboration its own unique richness and range of experience, knowledge, and talent to tap into.

But even the most compatible, peace-loving partners will argue occasionally as they co-create scripts. And that's not a bad thing. Disagreement is an integral and invaluable part of the collaborative process. It's so crucial that Andrew Reich recommends looking for "someone you've had arguments with or someone you know you can settle things with without throwing tantrums. If you're casual friends, how are you going to deal with each other in an argument?"

This may sound like a minor thing to consider when choosing a partner, but it's the intricate interpersonal stuff that comes from knowing your partner, your relationship, and yourself. Peter Tolan, on the other hand, claims he *can't* argue. He can't even bring himself to say, "No, that's not good." He considers this his greatest weakness as a collaborator. "You've got to be able to say, 'Here's why this doesn't work.' And you've got to hope, too, that the other person is open to hearing that." Tolan admires writing partners like Harold Ramis who argue with grace and wit. "We had a very playful collaboration," Tolan says.

But the Queen of Soul is right: at the end of the day, it's r-e-s-p-e-c-t that matters most. We ought to know. We went from zero to sixty on the issue — from contempt to respect. And only after we hit respect could we write together. "That's the most important thing about a writing partner," asserts Ted Elliott (*Shrek, Pirates of the Caribbean*). "Find a writer you respect, whose abilities you envy — and hope he or she feels the same about you. You should both feel like you're getting the better part of the deal."

In the end, collaboration — like love, friendship, or film — is experiential. No one, not even close friends or spouses or family members, can know if writing together will work until they try it. Like Andrew Reich and Ted Cohen when they brainstormed their first script. "All of a sudden, Ted said something, and I said, 'Then we could do *this*.' And he said, 'We could do this and *this*.' Funny ideas started flowing, and it just felt like *wow*, this is really a good idea! And *boy* is this more fun than sitting by myself trying to write. With Ted it just clicked."

So choose the most promising partner you can and see if it clicks when you work together. See if you say, *"Wow."* That's the real acid test. The journey of collaboration begins with one script.

···

How do I acquire the rights to a book I want to adapt into a screenplay?

DR. LINDA SEGER: If the book is older than the early 1900s, you can do whatever you want with it. If the book has been written since the early 1900s, you have to find out who owns the rights to it, and then option the material. If it's well known, the option might be a million dollars; if it's not well known, the option might be $10. You can contact the publisher's Rights and Permissions Department to find out who has the rights.

Then, you have to decide whether to try to sell this with a treatment, or write the script and then try to sell that. If you can get an agent, great, but if your option is for just six months or one year, you don't want to spend your entire option period trying to get an agent. So before you option the book, it might be good to have some kind of a marketing plan about how you're going to do this.

Since most books are optioned by a studio or a production company, if you do it as a writer, you have to be a good strategist. And hopefully, if you only do a treatment, you'll have some sample scripts to prove that you can write the script.

···

Where should a writer focus first in attempting to sell his script?

L. Cowgill: When you have a script that's finished and you feel is wonderful, you have to go everywhere and anywhere to get your script into the hands of someone who will help you. If you're not in LA or NY, or somewhere where they develop and buy screenplays, then you need to get there. Here in LA, everyone knows someone. You need to find out who knows someone who can help you get to an agent or manager.

One piece of valuable advice I was given early on is to always keep a copy of your latest script in your car, and if you can, on your person. You never know who you're going to meet, and if you can press the flesh and put the script into someone's hands personally, it's better than having them give you an address and having to trust the mailroom. The personal contact is important, as long as you can make yourself memorable in a good way.

I've finished my spec script, entered a couple of contests, and sent out a zillion query letters — and nothing has happened. What do I do next?

HOWARD MEIBACH: What you need to do next is what I like to call "selling your screenplay outside the box." Start by contacting low-level assistants at the agencies and production companies. They don't get much attention, and many are looking for brownie points to move up the company's totem pole. Find out who they are by calling the companies or looking in the *Hollywood Creative Directory* (www.hcdonline.com).

Next, contact up-and-coming video and commercial directors. Studios love these guys because they work fast and cheap. Finding them can take a little work, but it may well be your way in, so it's time well spent. You'll need the name of the ad agency or production company that made the commercial or video, which you can find by sifting through advertising, music, and video magazines at the library. If it's a commercial director you are seeking, you might also contact the company that makes the product and ask them the name of their ad agency. Once you track down this company, get the name of the director and his or her contact info. If the company only wants to give you the name of an agent, see if they'll forward a letter to the director. If they refuse, write to the agent, but don't expect much. If you can get a manager contact, that's often a better bet since managers are often more open to new opportunities than an agent. An agent is usually about fielding offers while a manager is about guiding a career. But never just send someone your script unsolicited. It's not the way Hollywood does business and your work will inevitably go unread.

You can also contact straight-to-video or low-budget feature folks. Go to your local video store and look at the backs of boxes of movies you've never heard of. You know, the kind of flicks that have Wings Hauser in the lead. Get the name of the production company that produced it and write to the movie's writer, director, or producer in care of the company. Or, you can call the company first, ask for an assistant and see if they'll forward your letter. This might be better if you're good on the phone. Like with the video and commercial directors, the people who work on lower budget films and straight-to-video releases are more likely to read your query and respond. Even if you have a big budget screenplay, you should still contact them. They might read it and suggest someone in the biz who can help you, like their agent or manager.

Some of the director who work in the lower budget arena can also be contacted through the Directors Guild of America (DGA). You should get a copy of the latest "Directory of Members." You don't have to be a member to buy a copy. (Contact the Guild at 310-289-2000.) All DGA members are listed in the; how much additional info is included depends on how much in demand that director is. A few listings even include a home phone number, but I don't recommend you call. Write first. If no office or home address is listed, write to the manager or attorney. If their rep's name is listed with no address or phone number, refer to the Hollywood Creative Directory's *Hollywood Representation Directory* (www.hcdonline.com).

If no contact info is listed — just the director's name — you might consider sending the letter in care of the Directors Guild, and having them forward it. Or, at least, they say they will. Contact them on the best way to go about this. But don't send them 100 letters or they'll think you're a potentially dangerous pest and won't want to help you. Also, again, your best chance is to contact directors who are new to features or who work in the low-budget arena and might want to break out. Stay away from the big guys like Ridley Scott and Ron Howard. In general, it's a waste of time and will only lead to disappointment when they don't respond. Sure, you might get lucky, but the odds of anything happening this way are against you. Play the percentages, and it might pay off.

BUZZ WORD

Preem – A dual-purpose *Variety* term: (n.) An opening-night or premiere performance; (v.) to show a completed film for the first time: "Several of the pic's stars were on hand for the preem," or, "The pic will preem on Dec. 18."

What is the difference between a professional and an amateur script?

L. Cowgill: What separates professional screenplays that get turned into successful movies from amateur screenplays is this: A professional's scripts are based on strong, simple story lines that are well developed and well plotted. Characters feel full and real, with emotional lives; the action has weight and meaning. Amateur screenplays are generally over-plotted in terms of action and underdeveloped in terms of character and emotion. Amateurs tend to focus on the action — what characters *do* — and leave the emotion — what characters *feel* — off the page. Amateur scripts feel flat and confused, and because so much happens, the significance is lost.

How should I format a spec script for maximum impact and salability?

DAVID TROTTIER: There has been a lot of talk lately about the new spec formatting style. Throughout the 1990s, there has been a movement toward "lean and clean" screenwriting: shorter screenplays, shorter paragraphs, shorter speeches, more white space, and the omission of technical instructions. It should come as no surprise that this gradual evolution continues to refine spec style. Let's take a quick look at where things stand at this moment in time.

What's Forbidden: Do not write CONTINUED at the top and bottom of each page. Do not write "continuing" or "CONT'D" as a parenthetical when a character continues his or her dialogue after a paragraph of narrative description. Do not number your scenes. I realize this may mean disabling your software, but that's because much of the available software is designed to format shooting scripts, while you most likely are writing a spec script.

Avoid Camera Directions: ANGLE ON, CLOSE ON, POV, PAN, DOLLY WITH, TRUCK, ANOTHER ANGLE, ZOOM, PULL BACK TO REVEAL, ZIP PAN, CRANE SHOT, ECU, WE SEE, and so on. Avoid editing directions: CUT TO, DISSOLVE TO, IRIS, WIPE. Notice that I use the word *avoid*. Avoid means to only use a technical direction when absolutely necessary to move the story forward. That might be two or three times in a screenplay. Remember, you are writing the story, not directing the movie.

MORE: In the past, when dialogue continued from the bottom of one page to the top of the next, you typed MORE in parenthesis below the dialogue, and then typed "cont'd" in parenthesis next to the character's name at the top of the next page. You still do. But only when you absolutely have to. Ideally, your dialogue should be so lean that you don't have to use MORE at all. Just move the entire dialogue block to the top of the next page or cheat a little on your bottom margin to get that last line in at the bottom of the page. Warning: Do not cheat on your left and right script margins and dialogue margins.

Parentheticals: You may have read that you should use actor's instructions sparingly — that you should not direct the actor in saying his or her lines unless the subtext is unclear. You've may have also read that since executives only read dialogue or just a few pages, that you should include some action as a parenthetical to help improve the read. There is truth in both statements. Let's be honest, executives are getting younger, often lack a creative background, and are being asked to read more. The result is that they read less. But readers — professional story analysts — read everything, after which they make their recommendation to the executive or producer. It's that recommendation that places your script in the running for a deal. In view of that, continue to use parentheticals sparingly, but consider taking occasional opportunities to add a line of action — say, three to four words — as a parenthetical if doing so adds movement to the scene or a greater sense of the character's emotions. And don't be afraid to write brief description. Film is still a primarily visual medium.

Length: Try to keep your screenplay within 110 pages, with 120 being the max — about 100 pages for a comedy and 105 for a drama. Paragraphs of narrative description should not exceed four lines. As a general rule, each paragraph should focus on an image, action, or story beat. Thus, paragraphs will often be only a line or two in length. Include specific details, but only details that reveal character or move the story forward. You create atmosphere or mood by the descriptive words you choose.

Capitalization: In your narrative description, capitals should only be used for a character's first appearances and important sounds. Do not cap props or other important words. If you must add a technical direction, then that would also appear in caps. Avoid the use of caps because it makes a script more difficult to read. Do not name specific pieces of music unless you own the rights to them or they are in the public domain.

Dialogue: Lines should not exceed three and a half inches in width. Ideally, dialogue should consist of one or two lines, maybe three. And yes, of course: There are exceptions to everything.

Author's Intrusion: Generally, you should stay out of the script. Shane Black made "author intrusions" hip. Here's just one example from page 91 of *The Last Boy Scout*: "Remember Jimmy's friend HENRY, whom we met briefly near the opening of the film? Of course you do, you're a highly paid reader or development executive." Shane Black can get away with that — you and I cannot. But having a personal writing style can add a lot to the read. I loved reading *Romancing the Stone*. The first line begins, "A size 16-EE boot kicks through the door...." I came away thinking that Diane Thomas had a lot of fun writing that story. I certainly had a lot of fun reading it.

What You *Can* Use: Use MONTAGE, SERIES OF SHOTS, INSERT, INTERCUT (usually for phone conversations), FLASHBACK, and SUPER. Use these for dramatic or comedic purposes, or for clarity or ease of reading; do not use them to dress up the script. I have a copy of the original *Basic Instinct* spec script by Joe Eszterhas — the one he sold for $3 million. There is not a single DISSOLVE, CUT TO, ANGLE ON, SERIES OF SHOTS, or fancy technique in his entire 107-page script. Only scene headings (slug lines), description, and dialogue — that's it. His focus is on telling a story through clear, lean, unencumbered writing.

The Bottom Line: Keep in mind that your audience is the reader of your script rather than a ticket-buying, popcorn-consuming audience, and that he or she is weary of reading scripts; don't encumber his or her read with technical directions. Just let the story flow like a river. That river will flow if you use visual, clear, and concrete language that directs the eye without directing the camera, and touches the heart without dulling the senses.

BUZZ WORD

Slug line – Adapted from newspaper use, in a script it refers to the first line of a scene that identifies all the most important information to the camera: interior or exterior, day or night, location, etc.

Finally, don't get paranoid about formatting rules. The story is the thing. Readers don't really care if you indent ten spaces or twelve spaces for dialogue, just so long as it looks "about right," has a clean appearance, and — most importantly — reads well. Hopefully, your lean script will earn you a fat check.

. . . .

How old is too old to be a screenwriter?

D.B. GILLES: Raymond Chandler wrote his first screenplay at fifty-six, and didn't even publish his first novel until he was fifty-one. For the record, he wrote the original screenplays for *Double Indemnity* and *Strangers on a Train*. In 1939, after F. Scott Fitzgerald's career as a novelist had faltered, he needed money fast. He went to Hollywood and found work as a screenwriter. He was forty-three years old. William Faulkner wrote his first screenplay at forty-eight. Joseph Mankiewitz (who, incidentally, rewrote Fitzgerald) was well over thirty-five when he wrote *All About Eve*.

As far as contemporary screenwriters: William Goldman is in his early seventies, David Mamet is in his late fifties, The Coen brothers are fortyish; and the Academy Award-winning writers of *Shakespeare In Love*, Tom Stoppard and Marc Norman, are no spring chickens, with a combined age over 120.

But these guys all fall under the category of "established" screenwriters. They've been around, and it's been awhile since they fell under the category of "young" screenwriters. So maybe the rules don't count for them. There's nothing like a track record to get a pitch meeting, a script read, and a deal.

So the more relevant question has to do not with the plight of established screenwriters, but with the new screenwriter with just a few miles on him or her. And when I use the term "new" I don't limit that to the older person who starts his first screenplay tomorrow. I'm also including that huge pool of hearty souls who've been writing screenplays for years and years, or even decades, without getting so much as a foot in the door.

It's getting that foot in the door that leads me to the two things older screenwriters have going against them — the Big A's — Ageism and Access.

The ageism factor is pretty easy to understand. Somehow, older and presumably wiser isn't necessarily better or smarter. In Hollywood-think, a twenty-three-year-old will write a more commercially viable script than a forty-three-year-old or fifty-three-year-old. That might be right, if the plot has to do with high school or college kids (*American Pie*, *Road Trip*, or any Freddy Prinze, Jr. movie), but when it comes to stories with depth and weight, I think it's fair to say that age and life experience can easily supercede youth and inexperience.

Not that screenwriters over thirty-five aren't capable of writing dumb, inane, and just plain awful scripts. And don't assume for one second that there aren't young screenwriters who've written wonderful, complex, smart, wise-beyond-their-years scripts. There's a moment in *Finding Forrester* in which Sean Connery reacts in awe upon learning that the gifted young writer played by Rob Brown is only sixteen. I know that feeling. On more than one occasion I've been blown away by the work of several of the young writers who've studied with me.

But the fact remains, the older a screenwriter — or any writer — gets, the better he or she gets. The same applies to lawyers, chefs, actors, or blacksmiths. Energy and enthusiasm are replaced by skill. Guessing at what life is like is replaced by living it. Why shouldn't someone who starts writing screenplays at thirty-seven be given the benefit of the doubt that she will write a good one?

The age thing is a problem for the new, but not youthful screen-writer. And it's exacerbated by the second obstacle: access, or lack there-of. If you're young (and I'll qualify that as being twenty-seven or under) or if you're youngish (say, twenty-eight to about thirty-five) you have a better shot at gaining access largely because of your physical appearance.

Younger screenwriters don't have to be afraid of meetings with producers and even agents. But the older screenwriter — by virtue of a touch (or a lot) of gray, crows feet and a mid-life bulge — risks turning potential dealmakers off simply because you'll be perceived as old. There's a peculiar kind of thinking in Hollywood that if you're older and haven't sold a script or had one made that somehow you can't possibly be any good.

And with so many universities and colleges offering screenwriting programs, more and more students are enrolling in them and coming out with BAs in scriptwriting. If a student goes to the right school, he will be pursued by agents and producers before he even graduates.

Let's get back to the person who decides to write his or her first script at thirty-seven. Or forty-six. Or fifty-eight. If you're a young thirty-seven and can pass for say, thirty, then you've got no problems. If you're a youthful forty-six, in good shape, and with a full head of hair — again, no problem. But if you're out of shape, balding, and are an overall physical wreck — you may have problems. Not with someone reading your script. But when someone calls you for a meeting. That is when it can get uncomfortable.

I've talked to agents about their policies of taking on clients, and producers about screenwriters they want to work with. They will all say that age isn't an issue — that all they care about is a good script with good writing and a good story. This is why it's to your advantage to get an agent first. The agent can send out your script and *nobody will have* to know that you have children in college or that you're about to become a grandmother. If you're a high-end Baby Boomer and not in the best of shape, try not to meet the agent in person before he or she has read your script. There will be a predisposition to judge you as being too out-of-touch to have written anything commercial. And with regard to those screenwriters in their thirties and forties who've been at it for a long time, there's always that little predisposition of people in the industry to assume that if you were any good you would've made it by now.

On the other hand, let's say you manage to get an agent to read your screenplay and she loves it enough to want to represent you — and *then* she meets you. The age factor might not be a factor if she thinks she can sell your work. Your age only becomes a factor if, as a result of having your script sent out to production companies and studios, people want to meet with you.

If they liked your script enough to overlook the fact that you're not a twenty-one-year-old student in UCLA's Screenwriting Program, they may overlook your age altogether. Or, if your script is so good and fresh and original. Or, if they like you and your attitude and personality and general disposition. Or if they are your age. Or older. To a producer in his early thirties, a screenwriter in his late forties might be perceived as a threat. Without getting too psychological, there might be a father figure or older brother thing going on. But to a producer in his sixties, if you're "only" forty-five, you're still at least semi-young.

The fact is, no matter how old you are, what matters is still what's between the covers of your script. If you're thirty-eight or eighty-three and you've written a 118-page turd, your age has nothing to do with it. Plain and simple, you've written a turd. And if some twenty-two-year-old clerk at Blockbuster — with zits and a bad haircut, who still lives with his parents — has written a great screenplay that sells for a million bucks, so be it.

Is it better to be young and starting a career as a screenwriter? Sure. Is it maddening if you started writing screenplays when you *were* young and ten years have gone by without anything happening? Yes. Are the odds against you if you're over thirty-five and writing your first screenplay? Absolutely.

But that's all the more reason to try. Why? Because you're a writer, so you know that the best stories are always the ones when your hero triumphs over insurmountable odds.

....

Does the screenwriter bear any responsibility to the audience for what they write?

D. Rivkin: After the initial shock of 9/11, one of the first things I wondered was if there had ever been a movie where planes crashed into tall buildings. And, if there had been, how did that screenwriter feel about that now? How often have you heard on the news that a child or teen was involved in some unique act of violence because they were imitating what they had seen on the screen? How would you feel if what you had written inspired a child's act of violence, or a teen's copycat crime?

While a screenwriter needs to write stories that are real and believable, there is also a responsibility to be cognizant of the effect of *what* you communicate and *how* you communicate it. I was once given an assignment by a top network television producer to write a story that involved a unique method of murder. As I can barely bring myself to even swat a fly, this was not an easy assignment. After completing the writing, but before turning it in to the producer, I contacted scientific and medical professionals to be sure that the method I had written about, while plausible within the screenplay, could not be copied or duplicated in real life.

As you create the idea for your story and write your screenplay, it's important to be aware that you are planting indelible thoughts and images in the minds of millions of people. Before you complete your screenplay, be sure that these are thoughts and images you're comfortable taking the responsibility for. For example, a top Hollywood screenwriter suffering with throat cancer recently issued a public apology for making smoking an integral and glamorous part of his movies.

As you write, it's important to decide within yourself what you are willing to be responsible for. And if you are trying to make your screenplay more marketable, know that physical and verbal violence are not essential components to selling a screenplay. There is an increasing trend toward family-friendly films. In a recent year, not one of the films grossing $200,000,000 or more — and only three grossing over $100,000,000 — were rated R. A great story and a well-written script can succeed without including whatever you may someday regret. As a screenwriter, what you communicate will have an affect on individuals and on society. Your words can sow darkness, or you can think of your writing as a candle to illuminate it.

••

How do I turn my writer's anxiety into creativity?

DENNIS PALUMBO: An old deodorant commercial once proclaimed, "If you're not a little nervous, you're really not alive." Pretty sage advice, even though the only thing at stake was staying dry and odor-free. But there is something to be said for accepting and learning to navigate the minor turbulences of life. I'm talking here about common, everyday anxiety. The jitters. Butterflies.

This is particularly true for writers, whose feelings are the raw materials of their craft. No matter how mundane, the small anxieties can swarm like bees, making work difficult and distractions — like an impending visit from the in-laws, money worries, or that funny noise the Honda's been making — seem insurmountable

Then there're the more virulent, career-specific anxieties, shared by few in other lines of work: Your agent hasn't returned your phone calls. You're three weeks past deadline with the script. You have — dare I say it? — Act Two problems. In other words, you're a clone of the Charlie Kaufman character in *Adaptation* — bleary-eyed, unshaven, sleep-deprived, staring pathetically at the empty computer screen, hoping for inspiration and yearning for another cup of coffee and maybe a nice banana-nut muffin. A dozen nagging, self-mocking thoughts echo in your head: You're untalented, a fraud. You're getting old and fat. No woman (or man) will ever want to sleep with you again. Your life is over.

These kinds of feelings require work, to be sure, if only to be validated (and then gently challenged) by a supportive therapist, mate, good friend, or fellow writer who's been there and done that. These deeply embedded, childhood-derived, seemingly inescapable, "dark night of the soul" feelings can, in fact, be crippling, regardless of your level of craft or years of experience. And believe me, when it comes to these writer demons, we've *all* "been there, done that."

And, as I've said countless times to the writer clients in my practice, struggling with these doubts and fears doesn't say anything about you as a writer. Other than that you *are* a writer. Frankly, this difficult emotional terrain is where a writer lives much of the time — in a matrix of triumphs and defeats, optimism and despair, impassioned beliefs and crushing deflations. In the end, it's all just grist for the creative mill. And, believe me, this is equally true for both beginning writers and accomplished, battle-hardened veterans.

But there's another kind of anxiety that emerges occasionally in a writer's life: The kind of gut-wrenching, dizzying upheaval from within that throws everything you think you know into doubt and scares you to the very core. A shattering divorce. The death of a family member. A spate of sudden, inexplicable panic attacks. Terrorism. War. Then, what balm is there to offer — or to receive — that doesn't seem trivial or woefully inadequate? Catharsis and validation, the foundation of most psychotherapeutic work, feel like mere word games. Medication, while often clinically appropriate, seems at best an armoring against something primal that's working within you.

What is a writer to do with that level of anxiety? *Use it.* Because when all that's left is writing, writing is all that's left.

What kind of writing? Maybe numbed-out and shapeless at first — chaotic and unsatisfying. Maybe dark and ugly, or self-pitying and shameless. Maybe a blind, angry clawing at the air with words and images. The important thing to acknowledge, to accept, and to make use of is the fact of the anxiety — its weight, its size, and its implacability at this time in your life, for whatever reason. It's there, as immoveable as a brick wall, as deep and fathomless as a sea. And, for now, it isn't going anywhere.

So you, the writer, must ask yourself this question: Is there a character in the story I'm working on who feels such anxiety, who feels as overwhelmed, as out of control, as terrified as I do? If so, plunge headlong into writing the hell out of that character, giving him or her your voice, your fears, your worries. Create situations and scenes in which these anxieties are dramatized, exploited, "acted out."

Write monologues, rants, vitriolic exchanges between characters; let passions and behaviors emerge that may astound or alarm you, that stretch or distort or even demolish the narrative you've been working with. These problems can all be dealt with, deleted, perhaps even woven into the story later, in the cool light of day, when you have some kind of perspective. Because to be truly in the eye of the emotional storm — to create from a state of anxiety — is to surrender any fantasy of perspective. In fact, in the purest sense, it's the ultimate act of creative surrender from which, out of the crucible of your deepest pain, you might discover a joyful, wonderful surprise.

If, however, you feel so impotent in the face of your anxiety that you can't even imagine utilizing it in this way, then write about that feeling — even if you have no characters whose voices you can appropriate, even if your fingers tremble at the thought of making narrative sense out of the inchoate feelings inside you.

Do this: Put those trembling fingers on a keyboard, *right now*, and start stringing words together that reflect how you feel, without context, or narrative, or character. Just raw feeling, in as many vivid, living words as you can call forth. Then look at what you've written. Feel whatever it is you're feeling. And write some more. Soon, I believe, you'll have a sense of the logjam cracking. You'll feel the urgency of creative expression, the palpable release of banked anxiety. Without judging what comes, without needing it to *be* anything, I think you'll find yourself writing, even if that's just defined, for the moment, as putting words down on a page.

Does the idea of this exercise itself make you anxious? Doesn't surprise me. We're all pretty scared of writing out of the very emotional space we'd most like to avoid or deny. It's human nature. But for those artists who have the courage to embrace their own fears, to stay conscious and connected in what seems like an ever more dangerous world, to co-exist with potentially crippling anxiety, and to write anyway, the rewards can be significant.

Moreover, when all that's left is writing, writing is all that's left. So trust it. Trust yourself. And write.

FOR THE SCREENWRITER

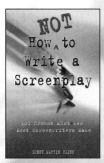

HOW NOT TO WRITE A SCREENPLAY
101 Common Mistakes Most Screenwriters Make
by Denny Martin Flinn

Having read tons of screenplays as an executive, Denny Martin Flinn has come to understand that while all good screenplays are unique, all bad screenplays are the same. Flinn's book will teach the reader how to avoid the pitfalls of bad screenwriting, and arrive at one's own destination intact. Every example used is gleaned from a legitimate screenplay. Flinn's advice is a no-nonsense analysis of the latest techniques for crafting first-rate screenplays that sell.
$16.95, ISBN 1580650155

THE SCREENPLAY WORKBOOK:
The Writing Before the Writing
by Jeremy Robinson and Tom Mungovan

Every time a screenwriter sits down to write a screenplay, he has to grapple with the daunting question of, "Where do I start?" The preparation time, or the writing *before* the writing, can be intimidating. *The Screenplay Workbook* is an instructional manual combined with proprietary worksheets, charts and fill-in lists designed to give screenwriters a better way to focus on the task of writing a screenplay. All of the organization is done, the right questions are asked, the important subjects are covered.
$18.95, ISBN 1580650538

FROM SCRIPT TO SCREEN
The Collaborative Art of Filmmaking, 2nd Edition
by Linda Seger and Edward J. Whetmore

Join Dr. Linda Seger and Edward Whetmore as they examine recent screenplays on their perilous journey from script to screen. In addition to completely updating and revising the first edition, the authors have added a substantial new section that is an extensive case study of the Academy Award® winning film, *A Beautiful Mind*, including exclusive participation by Ron Howard. In interviews with over 70 of the top professionals in the film industry, Seger and Whetmore examine each artist's role in making a great script into a great film.
$18.95, ISBN 1580650546

POWER SCREENWRITING
The 12 Stages of Story Development
by Michael Chase Walker

Michael Chase Walker offers a clear and straightforward framework upon which to build story plots. Standing on the broad shoulders of Joseph Campbell, Christopher Vogler, and others who have demonstrated how mythology is used, Walker brings passion, insight and clarity to a whole new range of story traditions never before examined. Walker offers a wide variety of alternative principles and techniques that are more flexible, adaptable and relevant for the modern storyteller. This book gives insight into the art of storytelling as a way to give depth and texture to any screenplay.
$19.95, ISBN 1580650414

PRODUCT CATALOG

FOR THE SCREENWRITER

THE COMPLETE WRITER'S GUIDE TO HEROES & HEROINES
Sixteen Master Archetypes
by Tami D. Cowden, Caro LaFever, Sue Viders

By following the guidelines of the archetypes presented in this comprehensive reference work, writers can create extraordinarily memorable characters and elevate their writing to a higher level. The authors give examples of well-known heroes and heroines from television and film so the reader can picture the archetype in his or her mind. The core archetype tells the writer how heroes or heroines think and feel, what drives them and how they reach their goals.
$17.95, ISBN 1580650244

WRITING SHORT FILMS
Structure and Content for Screenwriters
by Linda J. Cowgill

Contrasting and comparing the differences and similarities between feature films and short films, screenwriting professor Linda Cowgill offers readers the essential tools necessary to make their writing crisp, sharp and compelling. Emphasizing characters, structure, dialogue and story, Cowgill dispels the "magic formula" concept that screenplays can be constructed by anyone with a word processor and a script formatting program.
$19.95, ISBN 0943728800

SECRETS OF SCREENPLAY STRUCTURE
How to Recognize and Emulate the Structural Frameworks of Great Films
by Linda J. Cowgill

Linda Cowgill articulates the concepts of successful screenplay structure in a clear language, based on the study and analysis of great films from the thirties to present day. *Secrets of Screenplay Structure* helps writers understand how and why great films work, and how great form and function can combine to bring a story alive.
$16.95, ISBN 158065004X

THIS BUSINESS OF SCREENWRITING
How to Protect Yourself as a Screenwriter
by Ron Suppa

Practical tips for the writer, with advice on crafting marketable treatments, pitches, spec screenplays and adaptations. Plus important information on how to protect your work, get representation, make deals and more! Calling on his years of experience as both a buyer and seller of screenplays, Suppa conveys a taste of the real world of professional screenwriting to help writers survive and thrive in the sometimes messy collision of art and business.
$19.95, ISBN 1580650163

PRODUCT CATALOG

FOR THE FILMMAKER

THE DIGITAL VIDEO FILMMAKER'S HANDBOOK, 2nd Edition
by Maxie D. Collier

Maxie Collier's book covers the creative and technical aspects of digital shooting and is designed to provide detailed, practical information on DV filmmaking. Collier delves into the mechanics and craft of creating personal films and introduces the reader to the essential terminology, concepts, equipment and services required to produce a quality DV feature film. Includes DVD.
$26.95, ISBN 1580650589

THE INDIE PRODUCER'S HANDBOOK
Creative Producing from A to Z
by Myrl A. Schreibman

Myrl Schreibman has written a straightforward, insightful and articulate account of what it takes to make a successful feature film. Filled with engaging and useful anecdotes, Schreibman provides a superlative introduction and overview to all the key elements of producing feature films. Useful to film students and filmmakers as a theoretical and practical guide to understanding the filmmaking process.
$21.95, ISBN 1580650376

FILM PRODUCTION
The Complete *UNCENSORED* Guide to Independent Filmmaking
by Greg Merritt

Merritt cuts through the fluff and provides the reader with real-world facts about producing and selling a low-budget motion picture. Topics covered include: pre-production, principal photography, post-production, distribution, script structure and dialogue, raising money, limited partnerships, scheduling and budgeting, cast and crew, production equipment, scoring, publicity, festivals, foreign distribution, video and more.
$24.95, ISBN 0943728991

THE ULTIMATE FILM FESTIVAL SURVIVAL GUIDE, 3rd Edition
by Chris Gore

Learn the secrets of successfully marketing and selling your film at over 600 film festivals worldwide. Author Chris Gore reveals how to get a film accepted and what to do after acceptance, from putting together a press kit to putting on a great party to actually closing a deal. Gore includes an expanded directory section, new interviews as well as a new chapter that details a case study of the most successful independent film to date, *The Blair Witch Project*.
$21.95, ISBN 1580650570

To order, call 323.308.3558 • www.hcdonline.com

HOLLYWOOD CREATIVE DIRECTORY

HOLLYWOOD CREATIVE DIRECTORY, 51st Edition

Single issue $64.95
1-year subscription $164.95
2-year subscription $279.95

- Studios and Networks
- Film and TV Executives
- Production Companies
- Independent Producers
- TV Shows and Staff
- Projects in Development
- Production Tracking
- Selected Credits

HOLLYWOOD REPRESENTATION DIRECTORY, 27th Edition

Single issue $64.95
1-year subscription $109.95
2-year subscription $189.95

- Talent & Literary Agents
- Personal Managers
- Entertainment Attorneys
- Business Affairs Departments
- Publicity Companies
- Casting Directors

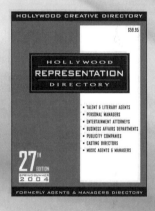

2004 BLU-BOOK PRODUCTION DIRECTORY

Single issue...$74.95

The Hollywood Creative Directory in association with The Hollywood Reporter is proud to present the *2004 Blu-Book Production Directory*—containing more than 200 product and service categories with thousands of listings. The directory is organized into 10 major tabbed sections that represent all the services and personnel necessary to take a film, TV, commercial or music video project from concept to completion. The *Blu-Book* also includes below-the-line craft professionals with credit and contact information. From camera rentals to sound stages to costumes to special effects to props to finding an animal for a production, it can all be found in this directory—truly "the Yellow Pages of Hollywood." Now includes expanded New York production listings.

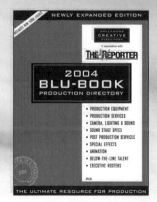

[This page did **not** have to be blank]

[Why I write…]

I write because I am always watching. And what I see all around me are characters, moments, details. An odd cadence to the way someone speaks or walks or breathes. A snippet of dialogue too good not to be shared. I write because some of the moments I see stay with me, refusing to leave, begging to be stolen and shaped and brought to life.

—Lizzy Weiss
Blue Crush

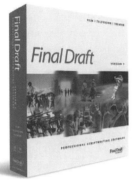